T0128947

And Then Came . . .

Nahjul Balagha

Peak of Eloquence
by
Imam Ali ibn Abu Talib

Translated by
Sayed Ali Reza

Mushtaq Haider Jaafri

authorHOUSE®

AuthorHouse™
1663 Liberty Drive
Bloomington, IN 47403
www.authorhouse.com
Phone: 1 (800) 839-8640

Published by AuthorHouse 01/03/2018

ISBN: 978-1-5462-2005-3 (sc)
ISBN: 978-1-5462-2004-6 (e)

CONTENTS

AUTHOR'S NOTES

Please read this before starting to read the book.

NAHJUL BALAGHA, in sermon 49, Imam Ali ibn Abu Talib says: *"Allah has not informed* (human) *wit about the limits of His qualities. Nevertheless, He has not prevented it from securing essential knowledge of Him."*

This book you are now reading helped me secure some of that essential knowledge of Allah's qualities that Imam Ali ibn Abu Talib was talking about though out the book NAHJUL BALAGHA - Peak of Eloquence.

This book sites translated excerpts which compile much less than ten percent of the original 680 page translation by Sayed Ali Raza. More than seventy-five percent of my own original metaphysical and personal commentary notes that are added to each Sermon are because perhaps, they were rather much too abstract for the mind of those people to comprehend thousands of years ago.

I most humbly request and ask that you please read this book with an open mind, in the spirit it was written and with a non-judgmental attitude. Take what works for you and leave what does not. It is a scientific approach for securing the knowledge. I sometimes indulge in my imagination to pretend that, perhaps, for thirty-five years, I was a student of the Imam Ali being trained to write and publish this book. May Allah Bless our Efforts!

La fatah illa Ali! – **There is no one like Ali!**

DEDICATION

This book is dedicated to the ZANIBIA ISLAMIC SOCIETY. (ZIS for short). It is Shia-Muslim IMAM BAR GHA (Church), incorporated in the State of California as a non-profit organization, based in Pomona, California, USA.

It serves a few hundred Shia-Muslim members in the greater Pomona Valley and surrounding areas. Its purpose is to teach the religion of Islam as taught as by the Prophet Muhammad (p.b.u.h) and followed by Imam Ali ibn Abu Talib (p.b.u.h.) and the eleven Imams after him.

The World Islamic Federation in London provides for this publication of the *NAHJUL BALAGHA* by the **Centre of Islamic Studies in Qum.** But we hope, to distribute this book all over the world, so that all the educated people of the world may be familiar with the teachings and sayings of first Imam of the Shi'ities.

May Allah bless our efforts.

November, 2017

ACKNOWLEDGMENTS

As anyone who has written a book knows, it takes a collaborative effort of many people. My thanks go to Kauser Zaidi for taking the original manuscript and skillfully recognizing the book within it. To Mr. Ali Hasan Naqvi for putting the words into a form that people could read. To Sabir Husain and his wife to loaning me the NAHJUL BALAGHA in the Urdu language to reference my book for accuracy. To my family for believing in the project from the start. To my agent Buddy Dow at the Author House fo helping me go through the 'Content-evaluation' and beautiful cover design process. My special thanks go to Mr. Nadeem Zaidi, President and Dr. Ale Raza, General Secretary of the ZIS to dedicate this unique book to this Shia IMAM-BAR-BAH in Pomona, California, USA.

CRITICAL ACCLAIM

FOR NAHJUL BALAGHA

Peak of Eloquence

By

Imam Ali ibn Abu Talib

Translated by

Syed Ali Raza

TESTIMONIALS FOR MUSHTAQ JAAFRI FOR THE BOOK:

And then came, NAHJUL BALAGHA

"The original Arabic book, 'NAHJUL BALAGHA' is translated into English by Sayed Ali Raza by the name of 'Peak of Eloquence', Imam Ali's collections is a literary masterpiece treasure; and for Shia Muslims, it is the most valuable and sacred text after the Holy Qur'an and Divine Scriptures. It consists of most famous sermons, letters and short sayings attributed to Imam Ali; cousin and son-in-law of Prophet Mohammad (P.B.H.H.)." Mr. Mushtaq Jaafri, a highly learned teacher and believer of Spirituality has made a wonderful effort to transform teachings of Devine Scriptures specially, teachings of Imam Ali into practical applications to surrender before the Divine Wisdom.

I sincerely hope that Mr. Mushtaq Jaafri's this endeavor will go a long way to guide men and women seeking path to salvation.

KAUSER ZAIDI (Retired Military Official)

And then came, NAHJUL BALAGHA

This book contains translated excerpts of sermons from Nahj al-Balagha written by Imam Ali ibn Abu Talib in the 10th century including published editorial reviews by some high profile clerics, professors and experts and more than 75% original commentary by the author Mushtaq Jaafri.

The book sites translated excerpts which compile much less that 10% of the original 680 page translation by Sayed Ali Reza.

Buddy Dow – Author House Publishing.

And then came, NAHJUL BALAGHA

"I want to start this work of mine with the selections from the book NAHJUL BALAGHA – "Peak of Eloquence". It is a work of the greatest thinker of the world, Imam Ali-ibn-Abu-Talib. This book contains such examples of chaste language, noble eloquence and superior wisdom that none but ALI can produce such a word—He was the greatest source of the religion preached by the Holy Prophet (AS)."

My own favorite SERMON 49 says: *"Allah has not informed* (human) *wit about the limits of His qualities. Nevertheless, He has not prevented it from securing essential knowledge of Him"*

NAHJUL BALAGA shares that essential knowledge.
MUSHTAQ HAIDER JAAFRI – Senior member of the (ZIS) Zainibia Islamic Society, Pomona, California, USA."

Publisher's Preface

NAHJUL BALAGHA is one of the most influential books of all times in pointing the way to spiritual freedom and personal achievement—of the spirit beyond comprehension by the human mind. There has never another book like it, nor ever can be.

The Centre of Islamic Studies in Qum, having already published the Arabic text of the NAHJUL BALAGHA, is honored to present the English translation. This book contains a portion of the Sermons, Letters, and *short* Sayings of Hazrat Ali ibne Abu Talib (peace be upon him), the greatest personality of Islam after the Holy Prophet Muhammad (peace be upon him) first Imam and the leader of Shi'ities.

Though the following book does not contain all the sayings and teachings of the Imam, it reflects the essence of one student's spiritual understanding of a few select Sermons, Letters and Sayings and is not intended to speak as any kind of religious authority on the subject. I'm not a scholar or a Moulana, just a student.

NAHJUL BALAGHA may be a good guide for knowing Imam Ali, but this book attempts to provide the *essences* of the teachings for the people of the East as well as the West under all conditions. The sayings of Imam are *not* bound by time or place, but are universally applicable for problems of life. **The Publisher!**

INTRODUCTION

My name is Mushtaq Haider Jaffri and I am a Shia Muslim currently residing in California USA. I believe that you will find that this book has a non-denominational, ecumenical approach to the subject under discussion.

NAHJUL BALAGHA is both a compilation of Imam Ali ibn Abu Talib's sermons, lectures, and sayings and a glimpse into Imam Ali's personality.

Translated into English by Sayed Ali Reza. Imam Ali's work is considered a literary masterpiece and by Shia Muslims *the* most valuable text after the Holy Qur'an.

The NAHJUL BALAGHA; "The Peak of Eloquence" is the most famous collection of sermons, letters, tafsirs and narration are attributed to Imam Ali, cousin and son-in-law of Prophet Mohammad (p.b.u.h).

This book contains only a few select sermons, lectures, tasfirs, and sayings of Imam Ali ibn Abu Talib that had the most impact on me.

You might think of this book as a "Reader's Digest" or the high lights of the NAHJUL BLAGAHA that had the most impact in the life of the publisher of this book.

Most chapters of this unique book will start with an actual excerpt from the sermon of Imam Ali ibn Abu Talib in the NAHJUL BLAGHA followed by my attempt to explain and share how I understand it. You'll find that this new unique book contains Imam Ali ibne Abu Talib's teachings blended with my own thirty-five years of research.

Imam Ali ibn Abu Talib says: *"Allah has not informed* (human) *wit about the limits of HIS (Allah's) qualities. Nevertheless, Allah has <u>not</u> prevented us from securing essential knowledge of Him."*

I believe that life is a series of 'turning-points'. Each turning-point occurs at a crucial moment in time and is an eloquent tribute to the hands of Allah in our life.

Several times an invisible force took control of events and by some miracle sent me more in the direction of securing essential knowledge of Allah—thus the birth of this new book – **NAHJUL BALAGHA!**

Mushtaq Haider Jaafri.

SERMON 1

Excerpt from the NAHJUL BALAGHA -
by Imam Ali ibn Abu Talib

SERMON 1. Description of the Creation of Adam.

"Allah collected from hard, soft, sweet, and sour earth, clay which HE dripped in water till it got pure, and kneaded it with moisture till it became glucy.

From it HE carved an image with curves, joints, limbs and segments. He solidified it till dried up for a fixed time and a known duration.

Then HE blew into it out of His Spirit whereupon it took a pattern of a human being with mind that governs him, intelligence which he makes use of, limbs that serve him, organs that change his position, sagacity that differentiates between truth and untruth, tastes and smells, colors and species.

He is a mixer of clays of different colors, cohesive materials, divergent contradictories and different properties like heat, cold softness and hardness."

In all honesty, when I read this description of the Creation of Adam, I felt as if Imam Ali ibn Abu Talib, had actually seen the creation of Adam, I mean how else can Imam Ali describe the creation of Adam with such clear details.

As I study the Holy Qur'an, I often wondered why did God speak of Adam and Eve's story in so many of Holy Qur'an's Suras—many times verbatim!

We are all aware of the story of Adam and Eve eating the forbidden fruit in the garden of Eden. I believe, that this 'act' of Adam and Eve constituted their disobedience to God, and I believe, that this really is wrong or sin (so to speak).

What I mean in plain language is that Adam and Eve saw themselves as having a *will* that was separate from God and they chose something that was different than what God had chosen for them.

To me, this 'act; showed a power-of choice thus, the birth of ego within us. In all honesty, I felt that this ego within us is nothing more nor lee than the Satan (Devil) in us to steer us from the path toward God and sadly, wins most of the time.

Imam Ali ibn Abu Talib said: **"The Allah** *asked the angels to fulfill HIS promise with them and to accomplish the pledge of HIS in junction to them by acknowledging HIM through prostration to HIM and submission to HIS honored position.*

"So Allah said: *"Be prostrate toward Adam and they prostrated except Iblis* (Satan). (Qu'ran,2:32: 7:11, 18, 17:61 50, 20:116). Self-importance withheld him and vice overcame him. So that he took pride in his own creation with fire and treated contemptuously the creation of clay.

So Allah allowed him time in order to let him fully deserve His wrath, and to complete (man's) *test and to fulfill the promise* (He had made to Satan)." (I'll talk more about God's promise later.) *"Thus, He* said: *Verily you have been allowed time till the known Day."* (Qur'an, 15:38, 38:81).

Therefore, Allah inhabited Adam (p.b.u.h) in a house where He made his life and his stay safe, and He cautioned him of Iblis (Satan)and his enmity. Then his enemy (eblis) envied his abiding in Paradise and his contacts with the virtuous."

The second chapter AL BAQARAH of the Holy Qur'an mentions the story of Adam and Eve and explains how Adam and Eve committed the original sin and separated themselves from God. Sin, the belief in the reality of our separation from God, seen by the ego as an act incapable of correction because it represents our attack on our Creator, Who would never forgive us; leads to guilt; which demands punishments; equivalent to separation, and the central concept in the ego's thought system.

The word 'sin' in the way I use it here is synonymous with the perception of separation from God. It's the ego's perception of separation from God The beginning of ego is the belief that we have separated ourselves from God.

This is what sin is: *the belief that we have separated ourselves from our Creator and have set up a self* (small 's'*) that is separate from our true Self* (God).

Sin is guilt. And, guilt *is* an expression of having sinned. Once we believe that we have committed sin (any sin), it is psychologically inevitable that we will then feel guilty over what we believe we have done or not done.

The key to remember is this: *Inside of us who we are as an eternal being meets the person who is here temporarily. Here the Spirit, the emanation from God, meets us, the selves we know. This is our point of convergence.*

(I'll talk more about 'convergence' later).The second chapter of Genesis of the holy Bible ends with Adam and Eve standing naked before each other, without shame. Shame is really another word for guilt and shamelessness is the expression of the pre-separation condition.

In other words, there was no guilt because there had been no sin. It is the third chapter where the original sin has been talked about, and that begins with Adam and Eve eating of the forbidden fruit. The act of doing that constituted their disobedience with God, and that really is sin.

In other words, they see themselves as having a will that is separate from God and that they can choose something that is different from what God had created.

And that again is the birth of the ego-self, the belief that sin is possible. So—they eat the fruit, and the very first thing they do after that to look at each other – and this time they feel shame and *cover* themselves.

They put fig leaves around their sexual organs and that became an expression of guilt. They realized that they have done something that is sinful and the nakedness becomes the symbol of their sin.

So that has to be defended against.The very next thing that follows is that Adam and Eve hear the voice of God, who is looking for them, and now they become afraid of what God will do if He catches them.

So they hide in the bushes so God will not find them. Right there you see the connection of the belief in sin – that you can separate yourself from God with the feeling of having done so, and then the fear of what will happen when God catches us with us and punishes us.

The way the ego keeps us guilty is to deny its presence in ourselves, sees it someone else, and attack that person.

That way we will be free of our own guilt. Indeed, as the third chapter continues, Adam and Eve were absolutely right, because does God punish them.

The interesting thing is that when God does finally confront Adam, he project the guilt onto Eve and says, *"I am not the one who did it, it Eve who made me do it."* (It is always the woman who gets it).

And, so Allah looks at Eve, who does the same thing and says, *"I am not the one who did it. Do not blame me, it was the serpent."* Thus we see exactly what we do to defend ourselves from of *fear of our guilt*: **we project the guilt onto someone else.**

Guilt will always demand that Adam and EVE be punished for their sin, so that when God does catches up with them He punishes them with a life filled with pain, suffering and sorrows and struggles the moment of their birth through the end which is death.

Imam Ali ibn Abu Talib says about sin in his sermon 16: "Beware that sins are like unruly horses on whom their riders have been placed and their reins have been let loose so that they could jump with them in Hell.

Beware that piety is like trained horses on whom the riders have been placed with the reins in their hands so that they would take the riders to Heaven.

There is right and wrong and there are followers for each. If wrong dominates, it has (always) in the past been so, and if truth goes down that too has often occurred.

It seldom happens that a thing that lags behind comes forward." **From the same sermon Imam Ali says:** *"He who have Heaven and Hell in his views has no other aim.*

He who attempts and act quickly, succeeds, while the seeker who is slow may also entertain hope, and he who falls short of action faces destruction in Hell. On right and left there are misleading paths."

The second chapter AL-BAQARAH of the Holy Qur'an also mentions the *story of Adam and Eve* and explains how they committed the original sin and separated themselves from God.

I would like to tell that story in my own words in way I understand it. Since I am a practical man, this is a practical book. Imam Ali ibn Abu Talib's sermons, lectures and sayings and philosophy are beautiful and poetic that can be used every day. As you read it, I urge you to use what works for you.

Imam Ali ibn Abu Talib gives us the description of the creation of Adam. Imam Ali says: "Allah intended to create *Adam* from hard, soft, sweet and sour earth, clay which HE (God) dripped in water till it got pure, and kneaded it with moisture till it became gluey.

From it HE (God) carved an image with curves, joints, limbs and segments. Then, HE solidified it till it dried up for a fixed time and known duration.

Then, HE blew into it out of HIS Spirit whereupon it took the pattern of a human being with mind that governs him intelligence which he (Adam) can makes use of, limbs that serve him, organs that change hi position, sagacity that differentiates between truth and untruth, tastes and smells, colors and species.

He (Adam) became a mixture of clays of different colors, cohesive materials, divergent contradictories and different properties like heat, cold, softness and hardness.

"Then Allah asked the angels to fulfill His promise with them and to accomplish the pledge of HIS injunction to them by acknowledging HIM through prostration to Him and submission to HIS honored position.

So—Allah said: *"Be prostrate toward Adam and they prostrated except Iblis* (Satan).*"* (Qur'an; 2:34; 7:11; 17:61; 18:50; 20:116).

Imam Ali says: *"that self-importance withheld him (Satan) and vice overcame him. So that he took pride in his own creation With fire an treated contemptuously the creation of clay.*

*So—Allah allowed him time in order to let him fully deserve His (God's wrath, and to complete (man's) **test** and to fulfill the promise He (God) had made to Satan."*

(I'll talk in more about the promise later). What all that means in plain language is that God told all the angels in Heaven that HE intends to create *Adam* from dirt of the earth. God said that when HE (God) blows Spirit into Adam's body he will slowly stand up before you. And, when *Adam* stands up before you, all of you are to prostate before *Adam*.

And, the angels in Heaven did immediately start to cast themselves down in humility. So---they all did prostate themselves before *Adam* as they were ordered by Allah to do so *except* iblis (Satan).

In the Western world the Satan is also called the Devil. (I will talk more about the devil later). Most my own life I have often wondered that just how did the **ego** come into being? I believe that Adam and Eve were the parents of the human race.

They were given a free will to choose and they deliberately chose something different from what God had chosen for them—thus, the birth of the ego. One easy way to let go of the ego is by observing it. Observation is the key to letting go of my ego at will. Only human beings are capable of observing the presence of God in all things.

So—they all did prostrate themselves before *Adam* as they were ordered to do so *except* iblis (Satan). It is interesting to note (to my own satisfaction at least) that Satan was one of God's oldest angels. Because of his devotion and worships to God, he was made the head of all the other angles of his group created by the evolution of fire.

The seventh chapter AL-A'RAF of the Holy Qur'an talks further about the Creation of Adam and the Defense of the Devil. God said to Satan, "What prevented you that you did not bow or prostrate before *Adam* when I commanded you to do so?"

Satan said, *"I am better than Adam. You created me of fire while Adam was created of clay or dirt. Fire is far superior to dirt."* When you throw fire, said Satan, it automatically goes toward sky and when you through dirt to the sky it goes to the ground.

As – S.V. Mir Ahmad Ali says: "Satan argued, saying he was created of fire and *Adam* of dirt, it will not be justifiable for a superior being to adore an inferior one. In fact, Satan insisted that *Adam* bow or prostrate him (Satan) in order to show respect for his old age and superiority over him.

But Satan, failed to consider the *three* factors in favor of the creation of *Adam*. First, he (Satan) was created of the evolution of the fire but *Adam* was created by God—HIMSELF! Whereas God had said: *"I made Adam by my hands and of my own Spirit."*

The second factor in favor of the creation of Adam from hard, soft, sweet and sour earth, clay, and then He (God) blew into His own Spirit is that fire is unreliable, for anything deposited with it is destroyed but the earth or dirt keeps in it anything duly endowed in it.

The third factor in favor for dirt being superior than fire is that fire is proud and arrogant and earth or dirt is humble and obedient and accepts being molded into any shape or form whereas fire does not.

The point I am trying to convey here is that the very first one who ever dared to start conjecturing with God was none other than the *iblis* (Stan). Conjecturing about God is a Satanic conduct and not acceptable hence forbidden. Speaking for myself,

I've often wondered about the story of the creation of *Adam and Eve* and about what prevented *iblis* (Satan) from prostrating himself before Adam when God commanded him to do so?

After all, he was the head of all the angels in his particular group, and because of his age and seeming years of tremendous love and devotion and worships to God he was indeed, regarded with great respect and admiration by all other angels in Heaven. In all fairness by my careful analysis of Satan's motive for refusing to obey God's command to prostrate before Adam,

I've concluded that it was Satan's own pride that made him disobey God. The negative emotion of **"pride",** was initially introduced by Satan. Satan, mistakenly really believed himself to be superior than *Adam* in everyway possible and wrongfully thought that Adam should bow before him because he (Adam) was younger and perhaps inferior to him.

The interesting thing about this Satan's.act' (to me anyway) of being so proud of himself is that this major negative emotion of

Pride never existed before. One thing Satan had learned was that when God wishes something or anything, then, HIS (God's) wish is always done no matter what. God says, *let it be done and it is done—because it is so—and so it is?*

Nothing and no one ever disobeyed God's commands. I earnestly believe from the bottom of my heart, that nothing (and I mean nothing) perhaps displeases God more than any act of angles or humans being proud of himself or herself, no matter how deserving you are.

The reason is that it was first invented by Satan. God was truly outraged. Then, God said to Satan. *"Since you have disobeyed my command therefore; you now don't have any right and privilege of living with angels in Heaven and being proud of yourself, thinking that you are superior to them."*

So—the story goes that God said to Satan, **"Just get out of heaven at once.** Now, Satan was a very clever and cunning angel and immediately realized that there is going to be no way out for him.

Imam Ali ibn Abu Talib say: *"Self-importance withheld Satan advice overcame him. So that he took pride in his own creation with fire and treated contemptuously the creation of clay.*

So, Allah allowed him (Satan) *time in order to let him fully deserve His wrath, and to complete* (man's) *test and to fulfill the promised* (**He** made to Satan).

12

(I'll talk more about God's promise to Satan later). I believe that life has a message for all those who, in their self-importance, forget that we can never control God, but we can align and flow with HIS will.

What I've learned in life is that *the joy of alignment with Allah, flows over into EVERYTHING I do—including the most mundane aspect of my day-to-day life.*

Coming back to our story of the Satan's disobedience to God for refusing to bow before Adam, Satan now realized that there is no way of the tailspin he was in.

So, Satan suddenly became very humble and said with great humility, "Dear Allah, You are a very merciful God. Isn't that true?"

Allah said: of course; I'm merciful.

Satan said: "You are a very beneficent God. Isn't that true?"

Allah said: Of course I am. What's your point?

Satan said again, *"You are a very kind God. Isn't that true?"*

Again Allah replied, "Of course I am. What do you want?

Three demands of Satan from God:

Satan then replied, *"Because of my many years of tremendous love and devotion to you and in return for all my worships to you, I am asking you to give all me my rewards right now!*

Allah said, "Go ahead and ask what you want and it will be given to you so you can leave Heaven at once."

How sad it is that the three things Satan demanded from Allah, truly became core reason why the human life on earth is often filled with pain, sufferings, sorrows and disappointments, from the moment of birth, through the end, which is death.

I believe that the three things Satan asked for became the main cause of all human sufferings and troubles in family and nations.

They are the truly caused of all misunderstandings behind our personal, professional, and social, relationships and even in our spiritual life. They are the real causes of all our fights among our brothers, sisters, in our religions and among nations.

The sad thing is that one of thing Satan asked for became an instrument through which Satan can work as an 'ego-self' which controls the bodily functions, directs the body, and asserts its desires and wishes upon us.

The 'ego-self' becomes the devil's advocate and whispers to us through the mind which is enemy.

*****

SELECTIONS FROM THE <u>SAYINGS</u> AND PREACHINGS OF IMAM ALI IBN ABU TALIB, INCLUDING HIS REPLIES TO QUESTIONS AND MAXIMS MADE FOR VARIOUS PURPOSES. Excerpt from the: NAHJUL BAlAGHA by Imam Ali ibn Abu Talib

2. Amir al-mu'minin, peace be upon him, said: "He who adopts greed as habit devalue himself; he who discloses his hardship agrees to humiliation; and allows his tongue to overpower his *Soul* debases the soul."

3. Amir al- mu'minin, peace be upon him, said: "Miserliness is shame; cowardice is a defeat; poverty disables an intelligent man from arguing his case; and a destitute person is a strange in his own town."

4. Amir al- mu'minin, peace be upon him, said: "Incapability is a catastrophe; endurance is bravery; abstinence is riches; self-restraint is a shield;(against sin); and the best companion is submission to Allah's (God) will."

SERMON 20

Excerpt from the: NAHJUL BALAGHA
by Imam Ali ibn Abu Talib

SERMON 20 - Death and taking lessons from it.

"If you could see that has been seen by those of you who have died, you would be puzzled and troubled. Then you would have listened and obeyed; but what they have seen is yet curtained off from you. Shortly, the curtain would be thrown off. You have been shown, provided you see and you have been made to listen provided you listen, and you have been guided if you accept guidance. I spoke unto you with truth. You have been called aloud by (instructive) examples and warned through items full of warnings. After the heavenly messengers (angels), only man can convey message from Allah (God). So what I am conveying is from Allah (God)).

Speaking for myself, I look at death and love death. I sometime indulge in my own imagination to see what kind of a place this world be in which to live if every human being visualized death as something that come **not** as one who obliterates, but as one who releases me from all pain and sorrow. I have learned to see death as a release from the pain of this earth and welcome it as a real friend.

For me, death is transformed from the grim reaper to the giver of new opportunity. The only thing that I can take with me— the only thing that is going to live and never die—is my Soul. Imagine, just for a moment, that tomorrow is the last day of your life.

What feelings does that thought inspire in you?. From this moment on you will need to be aware of the possibility and the certainty of death, and come to term with it. That means that most of the things you and I tend to focus energy on are going to begin to seem meaningless.

The beauty of death is its freedom. The key to remember is this: As you focus on your death, you will begin to focus on your priorities; on what is really important. There is an old cliché' that asks, *"If you had only one day left on earth, how would you want to spend it?* **Perhaps it's a silly question, but it's worth spending some time thinking about it.**

What I've found is that the most difficult thing is confronting myself. It is in those moments when I am free from distracting of the physical world that I have the greatest chance for upliftment.

Take every chance you get because you will live in this world, get married, have kids, spend your life in slavery to car payments and house payments, work eight hours a day, and die—and you can take none of that with you.

In the worlds of Spirit there is no time. However, in this world, time is a precious commodity. This physical world is a springboard for you into the higher consciousness.

Our bodies, minds, emotions, unconsciousness, and SOUL COME TOGHTER IN ONE PLACE, giving the best opportunity in the universe for growth and upliftment. **Since we don't know the moment we are going to die, so we can forgive ourselves and pray and focus on Allah at the moment of death, we'd better start doing it now.**

Arc you starting to see how precious the time you've already have? And how much more precious is the time that remains to you" *Keeping death in mind is not being morbid. It's being aware, that you do not have time to waste.* Perhaps you can see now why you don't have time to do anything other than focus on your purpose or intention.

The main point I am trying to convey here is that as a spiritual human beings, we do not have time to waste. Of course, as a regular physical human beings you have as much time as you want. The funny thing is, that as regular physical human beings you prefer to focus on the uncertainty of their life and worry about it, rather than look at the one thing that is certain: **Death.**

You are probably thinking that you'll have plenty of time to think all this over, and that you'll be a spiritual person another day. Welcome to the human race. Observe the slow evolution of human beings on the planer earth.

Sure, human beings have indeed, advanced enormously technologically, but as a human race we are still doing the very same destructive things that were reported in the Bible thousands of years ago. **Our thinking that we have all the time in the world prevents us from maturing.** Procrastinating is like pollution: *It's wasteful and sloppy and depletes our energy.*

How we die is so very important because it will be our last thoughts and our last feelings in this life. How we handle the turmoil of our existence is going to determine our placement in the Heaven when we leave here. So—our last thoughts and our last feelings in this life become very important.

I often remind myself that the life I've been living up to this point on this planet has been a *rehearsal* for death. Just think of it!

So I've make sure that I know how to get away from my body cleanly. I have to make sure that where I am going to place my consciousness.

This is why meditation, contemplation, spiritual exercises, prayers—all these things—are very, very important to the spirituality of an individual. What I've noticed is that the more

I dwell upon God and God's love and the extension of that consciousness to me, when it comes to those last moments before I leave this life, my own thoughts will be on that. **And, to that is where I will go.** So, it is a moral and religious statement, **"keeping death in mind".**

For me, as I go about my daily business, I try my level best to keep a clean mind and a clean body and clean emotions by watching where I place them. Most of us are afraid to die. But when we can contact the Spirit inside us, we find peace, and death seems as natural as breathing. **Life presupposes death. Death presupposes life.**

We as play game with ourselves; We pretend if we forget about death, death will forget about us. But as spiritual human being, I look in the face of death, and this frees me to focus on life. *While death is stalking me, I am stalking Spirit.*

One of the things I've learned in my own life is that we need to make peace with everyone in my life because everyone lives inside me. It doesn't matter if they are living or dead, or if I will ever never see them again. If anyone makes discord within me, then I've to make peace with them.

I start with my parents and try to make closure with them. I ask for their forgiveness and I forgive them. The moment I do that, the joy of alignment with my Creator God, flows over into EVERYTHING I do—including the most mundane aspect of my day-to-day life.

Recently, I read a story of a woman who went to visit a friend of hers who had only two or three days left to live. She said to the dying woman *"If I had few days left, I would be writing things to my children, videotaping,and dictating how I want the housekeeper to take care of the house, and how I want the nursemaid to take care of the kids. And, I would be leaving direction for my husband on how to get another really good wife."*

But then, all at once, that woman closed her mouth, and asked herself, "WHAT WOULD I *really* DO IF I ONLY HAD THREE DAYS TO LIVE." And at that thought she broke down and wept down and wept.

For the first time the immediacy of death struck her. She realized that the moment of death is not a time to be looking back, to be thinking about the past.

That is the time to live in the present. What I am trying to convey here is that the search for God isn't a race toward a finish line. As for the unknowable, it is true, "God is unknowable, but I know God." How can that true be? How do I recognize Allah? My answer is: **The best I can.** I've now reduced my own life to just one thing: *Seeking God 24/7.*

I do this through a process I have learned from my spiritual teacher who taught me this. **I call seeking Allah in every moment of my life as stalking the Spirit**. Or consciously show my love for Allah by repeating a self-suggestion (mantra) *Allah is unknowable but, I know my Allah."*

I repeat this affirmation 24/7. I also stalk death by rehearsing my last words on my deathbed: *"YA Allah, I did the best I could.!"* As I go about my daily business, I say, do and even think what will bring me closer to God regardless of any distractions, or whatever I may have to sacrifice for it.

My mind's fundamental purpose is to keep me busy with guilt, doubt, and worries and spinning around on the physical world. That is why my mind is my own worst enemy because it will always go against me in my spiritual pursuits. I observe my mind's thinking 24/7. Observation is the key!

How can I **observe** God when I am observing bad thinking of the mind, guilt, doubt, worry and resentment? I can't because God can only be found in 'goodness'. That is where I find God, goodness in nature, all things living and the universe.

People often wonder why do I stalk death while I am still living here on earth. They ask why do I rehearse my last words, "YA Allah, **I did the best I could?** I say to them because those words might help me stop the wheel of 84 for me. Then, they ask: What in the heck is the wheel of 84?

I say: the wheel of 84 means that a soul must pass through rounds of eight-four *lakhs* of rebirths. In Hindi and Urdu languages a *lakh* means one hundred thousand.

So— Souls pass through eighty-four hundred thousand rounds of birth and death.

Please understand that it is not my intent to give a long dissertation about the legitimacy of the wheel of 84. The modern public libraries are full of the books on this subject.

My only purpose here is to show how the rebirth process may be stopped.

Finally, I will lead you step-by-step through a process I've personally used for moving from the unknown to the unknowable to find Allah.

I've literally experienced everything I am about to share with you. It is a practical way to control the 'mind-activity' 24/7. The very first step in the process of moving from the unknown to the unknowable to find Allah to go beyond the limits of the human mind. The human mind, as powerful as it seems to be, it does have definite limits and it stops at the limits, as if the mind is dead or no-mind. You cannot use mind to find God.

The division between the left and the right sides of the Spirit is so delicate that it is hard to recognize the subtle 'alignment' energies emanating from the two sides of the Spirit. It is very difficult to see where the alignment energies are coming from.

These alignment energies don't obey any rules; it was up to me to use them properly to advance my spiritual intention. For me alignment with the Spirit was an ongoing challenge for me. The reason is that for thirty-five plus years,

I didn't even know that the Spirit has two sides, the left side and the right side.

Alignment with Spirit involves detachment from the material world; but it doesn't mean to hate the world. The joy of alignment flows into everything. We must live in alignment through the right side of the Spirit by loving, caring and sharing.

We must not live through the left side of the Spirit because our minds play devil's advocate in the left side of the Spirit; that is why the mind is your enemy. This will assist you in converging your Spirit back into alignment.

My spiritual teacher taught me that alignment does not happen in the known, it comes only in the unknowable and it happens as an *awareness* of unknowable. What I have discovered is that I can come into awareness of the unknowable by coming into alignment with it. For me, the *awareness* is synonymous with the unknowable.

That is why I say: *Allah is unknowable—but I know Allah.* Very simply stated, 'awareness' is becoming aware of myself as a soul and as a one with Allah not in theory but a living reality in my daily life.

Know this: when convergence takes place, for most, it is "grace" (me too).

Then, we come into alignment once again.

The key to remember is this: In the left and the right sides of Spirit, we find the known and the unknown. Both sides of the Spirit are necessary to maintain balance.(it took me more than thirty-five years to know this). So— what are the two aspects of the Left Side and the Right Side of Spirit?

The Left Side of Spirit can be imagined as the Intuitive, Emotional, Creative, Earthly, Dark, Path away from God. The Right Side of spirit can be visualized as Logical, Intellectual, Destructive, Spiritual, LIGHT, Path toward God.

Only through the Right Side of the Spirit, can you and I go into the unknowable and have alignment with it. If you are going into the Left Side of Spirit, you are, in essence going away from the unknowable—Allah. I must admit that it's not easy to live on this planet, simply because I have to live here, and live here, and live here.

And, some part of me says. "I'm tired, Lord." I know for a fact, that only God can release me. I also know that in order to win my freedom from the bondage from this material world, I've first to surrender to the unknown, which is Allah.

As I go about approaching the unknowable (Allah). I try my level best that my own 'ego' intention does not move my **awareness** out of alignment into the Left side and get stuck here for eternity.

I often sit down in meditation or spiritual exercises and close my eyes; have the intention to stalk the Spirit. The Spirit then starts to love me; and to be loved in me. I move more and more into Spirit, and a serenity happens in me. It is not a mental thing.

It is not what I think of as **"happiness." It is an energy field that is, by itself, absolutely whole and complete; it is called God.** When I experience this serenity it is as if I touch Allah. I feel I am the Beloved. I know I'm the Beloved!

What I've found is that most of us are stalking death. Those who are stalking the Spirit *bypass* the rules of death's game, slip past the bonds of death into the Light (Noor).

The most interesting thing I've discovered is that (and this may surprise you too),: **Death does not deal in love. Neither does it deal with health, wealth, and happiness; prosperity, abundance, and riches; loving, caring, sharing, and touching.**

It deals with obliterating your consciousness from this level. When we are totally in Allah, totally free of the fear of death, then at last death leaves us alone. We are no longer running from it so it cannot recognize us a its prey. We must be strong in our fearlessness.

Through prayer, meditation, contemplation, spiritual exercises, service, and love we conquer love. Speaking for myself, I try to look at death and love death. For me, death comes not as one who obliterates, but one who releases me from my pain and sorrow.

I've truly learned to see death as a release from the pain of the earth and truly welcome it as a real friend. Death is transformed from the grim reaper to the giver of new opportunity.

For me, the key to the proper knowledge understanding of the process of "death" is to know that I'm here on this planet earth for a limited, pre-set short time and not to live here forever, and ever.

I tell myself that I came into this world attempting to fulfill certain qualities within myself and go about it in many ways.

But I have a prime directive: *I'm here to find out who I am, and to find out where my home in spirit is, to go there in consciousness, and to have a co-creative consciousness with Allah. .*

I believe this is my whole direction and purpose on this planet. This is where my satisfaction and my fulfillment lies. *I don't belong here spiritually. I am engrafted into the body, perhaps that is why I I've such a hard time making myself do what I want to do according to my intention, because my intention only functions in the Spirit.*

I am not here to do what I know how to do. I am not here just to learn what I already know. I'm here to learn what I do not know and what I do not know how to do. But, the challenge is that I am here just for a short time, I mean what a hundred or more years life span and the next thing is that you lose the *fear of death.*

You see birth as the beginning of your physical body and death as a transition into something else. So the journey continues.

The physical body in itself is impermanent- its not going to last forever—so you lose the fear of death, that one way or another it will end and you focus more on the awareness of who you are as a Soul and as a one with God not in theory but a living reality in your daily life.

Suddenly, you begin to spend more of your time in spiritual pursuit instead of just reacting to the material world. You remain at peace and begin to align and *flow* with God's will.

You lose attachment to the material world. Don't get me wrong. You still enjoy good life but you don't make material things your permanent focus. You are also here to connect with people and make meaningful relationship, to enjoy life.

You still have your ups and downs but, you'll not be attached to the material things or have any fear of Death.

This way, you'll live more and experience life in much more deeper level. The funny thing is that once you lose the fear of death, you stop taking world too seriously.

You begin to look at life from the Creator's point of view. You begin to focus on life hereafter with the Creator Allah, who sent you.

*****

"When you have experience with Allah, you will realize that Allah is existence, and in reality, you don't live Allah, as much Allah lives you."

*****

SERMON 10

Excerpt from the: NAHJUL BALAGHA
by Imam Ali ibn Abu Talib

SERMON 10 – Talhah and az-Zubayr

"Be aware! Satan' has collected his group and assembled his horsemen and foot-soldiers. Surely, with me in my sagacity. By Allah (God) **I shall fill to the brim for them a cistern from which I alone would draw water. They can neither turn away from it or return to it."**

"1. When Talhah and az-Zubayr broke away by violating the Oath of alliance and set for Basarh in the company of 'A'ishah, Amir-ul mu'minin skpoe in these words which are part of the long speech. "

Ibn Abi'l-Hadid has written this in this sermon Satan denotes the real Satan as well as Mu'awiyah because Mu'awiyah was secretly conspiring with Talhah and az-Zubayr and instigating them to fight against Amir al mu'ninim, but the reference to the real Satan is more appropriate and obvious in accord with the situation and circumstances."

31

SELECTIONS FROM THE <u>SAYINGS</u> AND PREACHINGS OF IMAM ALI IBN ABU TALIB, INCLUDING HIS REPLIES TO QUESTIONS AND MAXIMS MADE FOR VARIOUS PURPOSES.

Excerpt from the book: NAHJUL BAKAGA by Imam Ali ibn Abu Talib

5. Amir al-mu'minin, peace be upon him, said: "Knowledge is a venerable estate; good manners are new dresses; and thinking is clear mirror."

6. Amir al-mu'minin, peace be upon him, said: "The bosom of the wise is the safe of his secrets; cheerfulness is the bond of friendship; effective forbearance it the grave of short-comings."

"It is narrated that Amir al-mu'minin, said in expressing this message that: Mutual reconciliation is the covering for shortcomings; and he who admires himself attracts many opponents against him.

*****

"In the last phrase, Amir al-mu'minin has described the consequences and effects resulting from self-admiration namely that it creates the feelings of hatred and humiliation-against others.

Thus, the man who manifests his greatness by every pretext in order to make himself conspicuous is never regarded with esteem. People being to despise him because of his mental condition in seeking self-conspicuity and are not prepared to accord the worth which he relay has, much less to regard him as he himself think to be."

THREE THINGS SATAN DEMANDED.

I would like now to share the three things Satan demanded from God in return for all of his many years of worships with love and devotion to Allah.

We are all aware of the story of the Creation of *Adam,* and how Satan refused to bow and prostrate before *Adam* as God commanded him to do so. And, how God dispelled Satan from the Heaven for disobeying his commandment.

The first thing Satan asked God about was about a change in the identity structure of his personality. Satan was created from the evolution of fire, and anything touched by fire is burned and destroyed.

The story goes that Satan asked Allah to grant him first wish by changing him into an ;invisible unseen entity (spirit) that cannot burn anything and unseen and unaware by the human eyes.

As I have said earlier, Satan is very clever an extremely cunning individual Satan, intended that by way of asking God to convert him into an invisible spirit that can no longer burn anything or anyone (humans), and as an unseen entity by human eyes, his (Satan's) intention was to be able to entry human bodies at will, at anytime and anywhere to humiliate them and seek revenge again *Adam, who caused him to be thrown out of the heaven with disgrace.*

It is quite interesting to note (at least to me anyway) that the negative emotion 'revenge' was first introduced into the world by Satan in human psyche.

I believe that the negative emotion of 'revenge' It is considered a ruthless enemy because it destroys ambition, clouds the memory and invites failures in every conceivable form. It kills love I an major attribute of God, I'll talk more about this later). The positive emotion of *love* is our natural inheritance.

The negative emotion of revenge discourages friendship, and *leads to sleepless nights and miserable, unhappy life to say the least.* All those who have suffered this ruthless enemy know exactly what I am talking about.

Revenge destroys the faculty of imagination and turns willpower into nothingness and it can ruin your own life. Through this negative emotion of revenge, Satan's first wish, to seek revenge against *Adam* for causing his severe disgrace and punishment from God,

Satan wanted Adam and Eve (the parents of human race) and all their children to live lives filled with pain and suffering, from the moment of their birth through the end, which is death.

The story goes, that God did grant Satan's first wish and changed him into an invisible spirit that could not be seen by the human eyes or burn them with fire.

The sad thing is that Satan, now as a being a creation of the evolution of spirit instead of the fire, could see us all the time.

Speaking for myself, as I look back on the history of mankind, I can't help but see that Satan did achieve his very first goal of bringing pain and suffering to the human race on the planet earth.

What I mean is that the world has been in a pretty bad shape, especially in this century, which is quite obvious to anyone who is looking around. I've been living in the United States of America for more than fifty years, and this country has hit a turbulent time in the world. The worse I've seen during the past half a century I've been living here as United States citizen.

Just recently, the Las Vegas police identifies Steven Craig Paddock as a man who opened fire from the 32nd floor of the Mandalay Bay Resort and Casino and killing more than 50 and injuring at least 515 other people in the deadliest mass shooting in modern US history.

The point I am trying here to convey here is that if you *think* that this man wasn't under the spell of Satan then, I say to you, think again!

So what to do to remedy this?

People are indeed, in great deal of trouble, and *some are being asked to contribute their particular talents and abilities to* <u>*undo*</u> Satan's first wish. I am asking you to contribute your particular talent and ability to serve mankind and try to undo Satan's vengeful wish. One easy way is to introduce the NAHJUL BALAGHA—the Sermons, Sayings, Letters of **Imam Ali ibn Abu Talib. So—what is the Satan's second wish?** You may ask: My answer:

Please listen closely.

Satan's second wish was that he be granted an everlasting life. Satan wanted God to allow him to never have to face death. This was Satan's second wish, to be able to live forever, and never die.

Of course, Allah totally rejected his second wish saying that every living being must taste death. I believe that God must have said to Satan that you had sinned by disobeying my command to bow and prostrate before **Adam**, and that caused his (Satan's) separation from the Paradise in the Heaven and the cost of all sins is death.

So—you, too, must die one day—there is no exception. But, as I mentioned before Satan is extremely clever and conning. He immediately got down on his knees and said with humility and head bowed down,

"You are a very just Allah. Isn't that true?"

36

Allah said, "Of course, I am just."

Then, Satan said, *"I do want justice. You just said that you'll grant my three wishes, and my second wish is that I want to live forever and never even have to die, just like all humans."* After a deep pause,

Allah said: *"Its true, I did agree to your three wishes and I cannot grant you a never-ending life, But I will allow you to live this life until the end of this physical world.*

(The Holy Qur'an the end of the physical world is referred to as the Day –of Judgment or Quamat). By way of this second wish, what Satan wanted to accomplish was to instigate *Adam* (and EVE) to commit a sin by disobeying God's command (like Satan) and eat the fruit of that forbidden tree and become liable being thrown-out of the Garden of Eden in Heaven in Paradise.

The point I am trying to convey here is the Satan hated **Adam** to the extent that he would do anything to have a revenge by having forced *Adam* and *Eve out of the Garden of Eden in Heaven.*

The sad thing is that he did win in his devious plans. Satan knew about the forbidden tree and he used it as a means to force **Adam** and **Eve** from the Garden of Eden in Heaven. Satan hated both to the extent to deprive the carefree living in the garden of Eden in Heaven.

It is quite interesting to note (at least to me anyway) that how Satan so cleverly used the negative major emotions of **hate** and **jealously** as tools for the human ego to keeps us away from God, spinning around the world, and not spend more of our time in spiritual pursuit instead of reaction to the material world.

I believe that hate and jealousy are the main cause of all troubles of the world. What I have discovered is that these two major negative emotions ensure that we are always stuck in the ego's wrong-minded thought system.

Hate paralyzes the faculties of reason and kills Self-reliance. It takes the charm out of one's personality and destroys the possibility of clear thinking.

This enemy of mankind kills the seven major positive emotions namely: *desire, faith, love. Hope, caring and enthusiasm, and assassinates the finer (positive) emotions of the heart.* It discourages friendship and eventually invites disaster in hundred different forms.

Let me further say this that jealousy is the weaker of the two major negative emotions namely: **hate** and **jealousy. But, make no mistake about it that jealousy discourages initiative and leads uncertainty of purpose in life.** It wipes out enthusiasm, and makes self-control impossibility.

Nothing will bring you so much pain and suffering and humility than jealousy. Only those who have truly

experienced this powerful enemy first hand can understand the meaning of this most powerful foe.

I earnestly believe that hate and jealousy are root cause of all human sins and the root cause of the perception of separation from God.

What is Sin? If you ask this question 100 people, you' probably get 100 different answers—and they will all be right in there understanding of sin.

The way I understand sin is that **sin, in essence is separation.** Sin is guilt. Guilt is an expression of having sinned meaning doing something that isn't right. Once we believe that we have committed a sin (any sin) it is psychologically inevitable that we will feel guilty about what we believe we have done. Guilt is to feel guilty for what we have done or not done. It's as simple as that.

I often wondered that what really is ego? I mean **Here is the paradox. Allah has been there. And for the most part, we have been there. If we have been there, and It has been there, why are we not knowing that we are both there? My question is:**

What is the thing inside of us that stops us from know what is going on. We don't belong here spiritually. We are engrafted into the body. That is why we have such a hard time making ourselves do what we want to do according to our intention, *because our intention only functions in the Spirit.*

What I have found is that the beginning of the ego is the belief that we have separated ourselves from Allah. This is what sin is: *the belief that we have separated ourselves from our Creator God and thus, set-up a self (small s) separate from our true-Self (big S).*

The point I am trying to convey here is that: *By way of Satan's second wish, he was endeavoring to punish (so to speak) Adam* by trying to induce guilt in the human psyche as the expression having sinned. Guilt will always demand punishment.

Let's now look at Satan's third and last wish he demanded in return of his years love and devotion and worships to Allah. Satan was indeed, pleased that Allah had agreed to grant his two wishes and now he was ready to ask Allah for his third and last wish that would implement his plan of mass destruction against humanity.

Through this well-conceived plan, Satan would actually become the 'ego-self' within all human beings and *attempt* to control human thinking through controlling the human mind and thus the mind will play the devil's advocate that sits on our shoulder and whispers to us. Satan tells us all the negative things about the world, about others people, it tells us how bad they really are. Satan tells us the terrible things they do.

So—what was the Satan's third and last wish? You may ask. My answer: *Satan asked Allah to grant him the power to enter all human minds anytime, anywhere he wanted to take over their thinking mind.*

When Allah heard Satan's final wish, God paused for a while pondering on Satan's motive for his last wish.

Then, Allah said to Satan that: **"it seems utterly unfair that you be given the power to control human minds by controlling their thinking and render them quite helpless."** **Satan, again pleaded with God, going down on his knees** (so to speak) **and begging Allah to be merciful and kind and just to grant his final wish to control human mind.**

Satan knew that only through his ability to possess the human minds could he implement his plan of mass destruction and take revenge against human race until the end of time which is the Day of Judgment or the *Quamat*, as it is referred to in the Holy Qur'an. God finally broke His silence and address to Satan said:

"since—I've already agreed to grant you all of your three wishes no matter what, I'll go ahead and give you the power over human minds, but let me tell you and warn you too, that I will also give all human beings the power of choice to either listen to your whispers or to hear the small still voice within. Every human being will the absolute *free* will to choose.

Then, Allah said: *Let me warn you that human beings that love me the most ove all other things will never ever listen to you no matter what you have to say to them—and this is my promise to you"* **With these few short words from God, Satan was dispelled from Heaven forever.**

Now—Satan was eagerly in search of the ways and the moments when he will force Adam and Eve out of Heaven by his cunning schemes. I will talk more about this story later.

*****

SELECTIONS FROM THE <u>SAYINGS</u> AND PREACHINGS OF IMAM ALI IBN ABU TALIB, INCLUDING HIS REPLIES TO QUESTIONS AND MAXIMS MADE FOR VARIOUS PURPOSES.

Excerpt from the book: NAHJUL BAKAGA by Imam Ali ibn Abu Talib

7. Amir al-mu'minin, peace be upon him, said: "Charity is an effective cure, and the actions of people in their present life will be before their eyes in the next life."

1.   This saying comprises of two phrases:...

The first sentence relates to charity and Amir al-mu'minin has described it as effective cure, because when a man helps a poor and the destitute by alms they pray for his health and recovery from the depth of their hearts and therefore their prayer is granted and bring him cure. In this connection, there is a saying of the Holy Prophet that, *Cure your sick by charity.*"

*****

The second sentence relates to the disclosure of action on the Day of Judgment, Namely: the good and bad deeds which a

42

person performs in this world cannot be perceived by human senses because of the veil of the material elements but on the Day of Judgment when material curtain will be lifted they will so appea before the eyes that will be no possibility of denial by anyone.

Thus Allah (God) has said: *"On that day shall come out people* (from their graves) *in* (scattered) *groups, to be shown their own deeds. Then he who has done an atom-weight of good shell see it. And he who has done an atom-weight of evil shall see it."* (The Holy Qur'an- 99, 6-8).

*****

8. Amir al-mu'minin, peace be upon him, said: "How wonderful is man that he speaks fat, talk with a piece of flesh, hear with a bone and breaths through a hole."

9. Amir al-mu'minin, peace be upon him, said: *"When this world advances towards anyone* (with its favors) *it attributes to him other's good; and when it turns away from him it deprives him of his own good.*

1. "The meaning is that when a man's fortune is helpful and the world is favorable to him then people describe his performances wit exaggeration and give credit to him for others' credit as well, while if a man loses the favor of the world and the clouds of ill-luck and misfortune engulf him, they ignore his virtues and do not at all tolerate even to recall his name. They are friend

of him whom the world favors and the foes of him whom the world hits."

10. Amir al-mu'minin, peace be upon him, said: *"Meet people in such a manner that if you die they would weep for you and if you live they should long for you."*

1.   "To the person who behalves with others with benignity and mannerliness, people extend their hand of cooperation, they honor and respect him and shed tears after his death.

Therefore, a person should lead such an agreeable life that no one should have any complaint against him, nor should any harm be caused by him to anyone so that during life he should attract others and after death too he should be remembered in good words.

*****

Sermon 22

Excerpt from the: NAHJUL BALAGHA
by Imam Ali ibn Abu Talib

SERMON 22 – About those who accused him of 'Uthman's killing.

"Be aware! Satan had certainly started instigating his forces and has collected army in order that oppression may reach its extreme ends and wrong may come back to its position.

By Allah (God) they have not put a correct blame on me, nor have they done justice between me and themselves."

They are demanding of me a right which they have abandoned, and a blood that they have themselves shed."

"If I am a partner with them in it then they too have their share of it. But if they did it without me they alone have to face the consequences.

Their biggest argument (against me) is (really) against themselves."

Imam Ali ibn Abu Talib Says:

"They are suckling from a mother who is already dry, and bringing into innovation that is already dead.

How disappointing is this challenger (to battle)? Who is this challenger and what is he being responded to?

I am happy that the reasoning of Allah (God) has been exhausted before them and HE knows (all) about them."

"If they refused (to obey) I will offer them the edge of the sword which enough a curer of wrong and supporter of Right. It is strange they send me word to proceed to them for spear-fighting and to keep ready for fighting with swords."

"May the mourning women mourn over them. I have ever been so that I was never frightened by fighting nor threatened by clashing. I enjoy full certainty of belief from my Allah (God) and have no doubt in my faith."

"When Amir al-al Mu'minin was accused of 'Uthman's assassination he delivered this sermon to refute this allegation, wherein he says about those who blamed him that:

"These seekers of vengeance cannot say that I alone am the assassin and that no one else took part in it. Nor can they falsely witnessed events by saying that they were unconcerned with it. Why then have they put me foremost for this avenging?

With me they should include themselves also.

I am free of this blame they cannot establish their freedom from it. How can they detach themselves from this punishment? The truth of the matter is that by accusing me of this charge their aim is that should behave with them in the same manner to which they are accustomed."

"But they should nor expect from me that I would receive the innovations of the previous regimes.

As for fighting, neither was I ever afraid of it nor am I so now. Allah (God) knows my intention and HE also knows that those standing on the excuse of taking revenge are themselves assassinations."

"Thus, history corroborates that the people who managed his ('Uthman's) assassination by agitation and had prevented his burial in Muslim' graveyard by hurling stones at his coffin were the same who rose for avenging his blood.

In this connection the name of Tallah ibn Ubaydillah, az- Zubayr ibn al- Awwam and A'ishah are at the top of the list since on both occasions their efforts come to sight with conspicuity.

Thus Ali ibn Abi'l-Hadid writes this:

"Those who written the account of assassination of 'Uthman statethat on the day of his killing, Tallah's condition was that in order to obscure himself from the eyes of the purpose he had a veil on his face and was shooting arrows ay ;Uthman's house."

And in this connection, about az- Zubuyr's idea he writes "Historians have also state that Az-Zubayr used to say 'kill 'Uthman. He has altered the faith.

"People said, "Your son is standing at his door and guarding him, and replied, "Even my son may be lost, but 'Uthman must be killed. 'Uthman will be lying a carcass on Siraj tomorrow. (Sharh *Naj al balaghah).*

About 'A'ishah, ibn Abd Rabbih writes: *"al-Mughirah ibn Shu'bah came to 'A ishah when she said, "O' Abil'Abdillah, I wish you had been with me on the day of jamal; how arrows were piercing through my hawdaj (camel litter) till some of them stuck my body."*

Al-Mughirah said: : *"I wish one of them should have killed you."* She said" Allah may have pity you; why so"" He replied, "So that it would have been some atonement for what you had done against 'Uthman."(al-'Iqd al-farid, vol. 4 p. 204).

(The Holy Qur'an – Chapter Two, AL-BAQARAH – S.V. Mir Ahmad).

"And said We' O' Adam! dwell thou and thy mate in the Garden and eat ye two there from freely as ye two wish and approach not ye two this three lest ye two will be the transgressions!"

What that means in plain language is that God said to Adam and Eve that both of them live in the Garden of Eden and should eat freely all fruits of the Garden, as their heart desired. But HE (God) warned then against eating the fruit of this forbidden tree, and if they did, they should surely die.

The key to remember is this: God made two things perfectly clear to both Adam and Eve. First, they were not to eat the fruit of the forbidden tree. Second, they were to always remember that Satan is truly their enemy. Everything else in the Garden of Eden was there just for their use as their heart desired.

The most interesting thing (at least to me anyway) is the Allah being so kind, merciful and forgiving said that: *"Satan is your enemy."* To my own knowledge, Allah had never called anyone an enemy—perhaps the reason is that Satan would against Allah in our spiritual pursuits.

Every time you and I have made a resolution to do anything, from going on a diet to doing spiritual exercises, prayers, meditation or contemplation, Satan will come in and challenge you and I to demonstrate how much you and I mean it. The funny thing is that our minds plays devil's advocate inside of us.

Speaking for myself, this testing, doubting, holding back are essential, because they show me where I am going, they help me to define my intention, and they make me work for it.

I often compare the process of spiritual growth and expansion to climbing a mountain. As I reach each new level. I am tested (by Satan) before I can climb to next higher level.

The struggle to maintain balance between the right and wrong daily aspect of my day-to-day life is one way I get tested by Satan. About Allah's attributes and the negative qualities of Satan test me to see if I really mean what I profess; they test whether my spiritual house' is built on rock or sand (so to speak).

So—in order to come back to the story of Adam and Eve, and the warning of Allah not to eat the fruit of the forbidden tree in the Garden of Eden, they began to live a pleasant, peaceful and carefree life in the Garden of Eden in Paradise in Heaven. They did what they pleased. They ate whatever their heart desired. In a way, both were having a great time enjoying the fruits of the Garden in Paradise in Heaven.

Just as a footnote about eating the fruits of the forbidden tree, I sometimes visualize, or imagine or just pretend that both Adam and Eve, being humans, every time they came near the forbidden tree, they must have wondered why God had forbidden them to go near the tree?

I mean what made the particular tree so special or different from all trees in the Garden of Eden in Paradise in Heaven"? What would happen if they did eat the fruit of the forbidden tree?

Day by day Adam and Eve must have become more and more intrigued and curious about this particular tree. But they never ever dared to go near the tree.

I believe that the human mental state of 'curiosity', perhaps, came first into human psyche when Adam and Eve became curious about the forbidden tree. No one (angels or Jins) had never become curios about anything before. Whatever God said, it was done, no question asked.

Some Western scholars believe that this God's warning of not eating the fruit of the forbidden tree was just a test from God to introduce **'duality'** on the planet earth. God knew that Adam and Eve would fail the test. (as a *will* of Allah).

This way, Allah introduced the principle of the cause and effect; good and bad; love and hate; happy and unhappy; health and unhealthy; night and day and so on. We can only know something by its opposite.

Some Eastern mystics and thinkers believe that Adam and Eve's carefree living in the Garden of Eden in Heaven had made them dull, soft and idle doing nothing.

These spiritual masters of all ages believe that there is an *evolvement* pattern for our Souls in the human body. As humans, we evolve upward to into the God-force.

Everything is a lesson. Every action involving the law of cause and effect is a learning situation. It's the teacher. Some people say when difficult learning situations are brought to a person, it's the work of the devil, but it isn't even close to be being right.

This is really an opportunity to learn, to balance past actions, and to move on in the progression of consciousness. Our traditional concept of the devil would fit better in the area of obsessions or possessions.

One of my spiritual teachers used to say: *"Sometimes these actions can make you think* "the devil had me", because you don't seem able to control yourself or to learn and progress. But remember, if there is a sin, it's not in the Soul; it's only in the personality.

And even then, *sin* means "missing the mark" of expressing as the divine being that you are." The human mind has often put the Soul in such a bondage that it pushes the Soul back from the body.

Soul starts giving over control of the body to the mind (Satan). As it does this more and more, the person usually becomes increasingly senile. You think that they are getting old and know they are going to die soon. When the Soul steps back, the body dies.

It is said that people have lived to be hundreds of years old in the physical body because they didn't allow the mind to put the Soul in bondage. People who spend more of their time in spiritual pursuits instead of reacting to the material world seem to live much longer and can remain in peace.

SELECTIONS FROM THE <u>SAYINGS</u> AND PREACHINGS OF IMAM ALI IBN ABU TALIB, INCLUDING HIS REPLIES TO QUESTIONS AND MAXIMS MADE FOR VARIOUS PURPOSES.

Excerpt from the book: NAHJUL BAKAGA by Imam Ali ibn Abu Talib

11. Amir al-mu'minin, peace be upon him, said: "When you gain power over your adversary pardon him by way of thanks for being able to overpower him."

The occasion for pardon and forgiveness is when there is power to take revenge. But when there is no such power, then pardon is just the result of helplessness, for which there is no credit.

However, to practice pardon despite having power and the ability to avenge is the essence of human distinction and an expression of thanks to Allah (God) for bestowing this power, because the feeling of gratefulness necessitates that man should bow before ALLAH (God) in humbleness and humiliation by which the delicate feeling of pity and kindness will arise in his heart and the rising flames of rage and anger will cool down after which there be no urge to take revenge under the effect of which he would use his power and capability to satisfy his anger instead of using it properly.

*****

12. Amir al-mu'minin, peace be upon him, said: *"The most helpless of all men is he who cannot find a few brothers during his life, but still more helpless is he who finds such a brother but loses him"*

It is not difficult to attract by good manners and cheerfulness and to befriend them by sweet speck because no physical exertion or mental worry is required for this; and after making friends it is still easier to maintain the friendship and good relations.

*****

SERMON 64

Excerpt from the : NAHJUL BALAGHA
by Imam Ali ibn Abu Talib

SERMON 64 – About Allah's attributes

"Praise be to Allah (God) for Whom one condition does not proceed another so that He may be the First before being the Last or He may be Manifest before being Hidden.

Everyone called one (alone) save Him is by virtue of being small (in number); and everyone enjoying honor other than Him is humble. Every powerful person other than Him is weak. Every master (owner) other than Him is slave (owned)."

"Every knower other ham Him is seeker of knowledge. Every controller other than Him is something imbued with control and light voices while loud voices make him deaf and distant voices also get away from him."

"Every on-looker other than Him is blind to hidden colors and delicate bodies. Every manifest thing other than Him is hidden, but every hidden thing other ham Him is incapable of becoming manifest."

"He did not create what He created to fortify His authority nor for the fear of the consequences of time, nor to seek help against the attack of an equal of a boastful partner or a hateful opponent.

"On the other hand all the creatures are reared by Him and are His humbled salves. He is not conditioned in anything so that it be said that He exists therein, nor s He separated from anything so as to be said that He is away from it."

"The creation is what He initiated or the administration of what He controls did nor fatigue Him. No disability overtook Him against what He created."

""No misgiving ever occurred to Him in what He ordained and resolved. But His verdict is certain. His knowledge is definite. His governance is overwhelming. He is wished for at time of distress and He is feared even in bounty.

*****

A Focus Point

The information that follows may seem rather abstract. It's okay if you don't fully understand it.

Just allow your inner wisdom to absorb it. Keep reflecting on the issues suggested here.

You will find your understanding of them deepen more and more as you progress of the examples of chaste language.

*****

Recently, I was working with a worldwide organization called the *Movement of Spiritual Inner Awareness (MSIA)* which is based, in Los Angeles, California.

This movement was begun more that fifty-five years ago by a man named **John-Roger** who held the inner-keys to the mystical traveler consciousness. John-Roger once said something in his seminars that truly caught my attention and I would like to share with you because it talks - "**About Allah's attributes.**

*****

1. Note:

Allah is referred to God in the Western world

1.   (in Christianity and other monotheistic religions) the creator and ruler of the universe and source of all moral authority; the supreme being.

(A Talk Given on - Attributes of Allah. John-Roger D.S.S)

God Is Un-knowable but I Know God

"Your task is to build a better world," Said God, and I answered, "How?" "This world is such a large vast place, and, oh so complicated now, and, I am so small and useless, there is nothing I can do."

But God in all his wisdom said, "You just build a better you." For the past thirty five plus years I believed that I can use my own mind to find God. Never did I realized the universal truth that the mind has limitations and stops at the limit of the mind. One of my spiritual masters often said: "We are moving from the Unknown to the Unknowable.

Frankly, I had no clue what in the heck it means. Then, suddenly, it hit me like a jolt of lightening. Wham! It really dawned on me what this great spiritual master was telling me.

I reasoned that if I know something it is called the *known*, likewise; if I don't know something, it is called the *unknown* (simple right) but, this unknown can be known. And, finally there is what we can *never* know—*the unknowable.* So what this great spiritual master was telling me was that in order to find God, we are moving from the unknown to the unknowable, because God is in the unknowable.

What I am trying to convey here is that the search for God isn't a race toward a finish line. As for the unknowable, it is true, "God is unknowable, but I know God." How can that true be? How do I recognize God?

My answer is: The best I can.

I've now reduced my own life to just one thing: *Seeking God 24/7.* I do this through a process I have learned from my spiritual teacher who taught me this.

I call seeking God in every moment of my life as stalking the Spirit. Or consciously show my love for God by repeating a self-suggestion (mantra) *"God is unknowable but, I know God.* I repeat this affirmation 24/7.

I also stalk death by rehearsing my last words on my deathbed: *"I did the best I could, God!"* As I go about my daily business, I say, do and even think what will bring me closer to God regardless of any distractions, or whatever I may have to sacrifice for it.

My mind's fundamental purpose is to keep me busy with guilt, doubt, and worries and spinning around on the physical world.

That is why my mind is my own worst enemy because it will always goes against me in my spiritual pursuits. I observe my mind's thinking 24/7. How can I **observe** God when I am observing bad thinking of the mind, guilt, doubt, worry and resentment?

I can't because God can only be found in 'goodness'. There is where I find God, goodness in nature, all things living and the universe. People often wonder why do I stalk death while I am still living here on earth.

They ask why do I rehearse my last words, **"I did the best I could, God"?** I say to them because those words might help me stop the wheel of 84 for me.

Then, they ask: What in the heck is the wheel of 84? I say: The wheel of 84 means that a soul must pass through rounds of eight-four *lakhs* of rebirths. In Hindi and Urdu languages a *lakh* means one hundred thousand.

So—souls pass through eight-four hundred thousand rounds of birth and death. Please understand that it is not my intent to give a long dissertation about the legitimacy of the wheel of 84. The modern public libraries are full of the books on this subject. My only purpose here is to show how I may stop the rebirth process for me. Just think if it!

Finally, I will lead you step-by-step through a process I've personally used for moving from the unknown to the unknowable to find God. I've literally experienced everything I am about to share with you.

It is a practical way to control the 'mind-activity' 24/7. The very first step in the process of moving from the unknown to the unknowable to find God to go beyond the limits of the human mind.

The human mind, as powerful as it seems to be, it does have definite limits and it stops at the limits, as if the mind is dead or no-mind. You cannot use mind to find God.

The division between the left and the right sides of the Spirit is so delicate that it is hard to recognize the subtle 'alignment' energies emanating from the two sides of the Spirit. It is very difficult to see where the alignment energies arc coming from.

These alignment energies don't obey any rules; it was up to me to use them properly to advance my spiritual intention. For me alignment with the Spirit was an ongoing challenge for me.

The reason is that for thirty-five plus years, I didn't even know that the Spirit has two sides, the left side and the right side. Alignment with Spirit involves detachment from the material world; but it doesn't mean to hate the world.

The joy of alignment flows into everything. We must live in alignment through the right side of the Spirit by loving, caring and sharing. We must not live through the left side of the Spirit because our minds play devil's advocate in the left side of the Spirit that is why the mind is your enemy.

This information will assist you in converging your Spirit back into alignment. My spiritual teacher taught me that alignment does not happen in the known, it comes only in the unknowable and it happens as an *awareness* of unknowable.

What I have discovered is that I can come into awareness of the unknowable by coming into alignment with it. For me, the *awareness* is synonymous with the unknowable. That is why I say: ***God is unknowable—but I know God.***

Very simply stated, 'awareness' is becoming aware of myself as a soul and as a one with God not in theory but a living reality in my daily life. Know this: when convergence takes place, for most, it is "grace" (me too) Then, we come into alignment once again.

The key to remember is this: In the left and the right sides of Spirit, we find the known and the unknown. Both sides of the Spirit are necessary to maintain balance.(it took me more than thirty-five years to know this). So—what are the two aspects of the Left Side and the Right Side of Spirit?

The Left Side of Spirit can be imagined as the Intuitive, Emotional, Creative, Earthly, Dark, Path away from God. The Right Side of spirit can be visualized as Logical, Intellectual, Destructive, Spiritual, LIGHT, Path toward God.

Only through the Right Side of the Spirit, can you and I go into the unknowabl and have alignment with it. If you are going into the Left Side of Spirit, you are, in essence going away from the unknowable—God!

I must admit that it's not easy to live on this planet, simply because I have to live here, and live here, and live here. And, some part of me says. "I'm tired, Lord." I know for a fact, that only God can release me. I also know that in order to win my freedom from the bondage from this matcrial world, I've first to surrender to the unknowable, which is God. As I go about approaching the unknowable (referring to God). I try my level best that my own 'ego' intention does not move my **awareness** out of alignment into the Left side and get stuck here for eternity.

SELECTIONS FROM THE LETTERS AND PREACHINGS OF IMAM ALI IBN ABU TALIB, INCLUDING HIS REPLIES TO QUESTIONS AND MAXIMS MADE FOR VARIOUS PURPOSES.

Excerpt from the book: NAHJUL BAKAGA by Imam Ali ibn Abu Talib.

LETTER 57 – To the people of Kufa at the time of his march from Medina to Basrah Amir al-mu'minin, peace be upon him, said:

"Now, I have come out of my city either as an oppressor as the oppressed. In any case, to whomsoever this letter of mine reaches, I appeal to him in the name of Allah (God) *that he*

should come to me and if I am in the right he should help me; but if I am in the wrong then he should try to get me to the right according to his views."

*****

Excerpt from the book: NAHJUL BAKAGA by Imam Ali ibn Abu Talib

LETTER - 68 – To Salmian al- Farisi before Amir al-mu'minin's caliphate. Amir al-mu'minin, peace be upon him, said

"Now, the example of the world is that of a snake which is soft in touch but whose poison is fatal. Therefore, keep yourself aloof from whatever appears good to you because of its short stay with you. Do not worry for it because of your conviction that it will leave you and that its circumstances are vicissitudes.?

"When you feel the most attracted toward it, shun it most, because whenever someone is assured of happiness in it, it throws him into danger; or when he feel secured in it, the world alters his security into fear; and that is an end to the matter."

*****

LETTER - 72 – To 'Abdullah ibn al- Abbis- Amir al-mu'minin peace be upon him, said:

"Now, you cannot go farther than the limit of your life, nor can you be given a livelihood which is not for you. Remember that this life consists of two days – a day for you, and a day against you, that that the world is a house (changing)authorities.

Whatever in it is for you will come to you despite your weakness; and whatever in it turns against you cannot be brought back despite your strength."

*****

LETTER - 76 – Given to 'Abdullah ibn al-'Abbais at the time of his appointment as his Governor of Basrah. - Amir al-mu'minin peace be upon him, said: *"Meet people with a broad face, allow them free audience and pass generous orders. Avoid anger because it is a* **Satan. Remember whatever take you near Allah**(God)**, takes you takes you away from Fire (Hell).**

*****

And then came…..

NAHJUL BALAGA

First of all, let me tell you that I am in no way more special, more gifted, or more talented or even spiritual than you are. I am just like you and any others reader of this book.

I am on my own spiritual path and for over thirty-five years I did study with a whole lot of wonderful people, with spiritual teachers, and for me it's a spiritual journey and I am happy to teach you everything I know.

Over the past thirty-five years, I've sensed as if my whole life has been a long road to a spiritual path in a series of turning points. Often, I felt as if I seemed to be going in the direction I do not wish to go. Look back sometimes and retrace some early turning points in your own life and, you too, like me, will discover it is absolutely true for you.

The peculiar thing about all this is that these turning points in our lives are important, for each occurs at a crucial moment in—and are an eloquent tribute to the hand of God in our life. So look back sometimes.

You, too, will notice that at any given points in your life, an invisible force, or Higher Power (call it whatever you want) took control of events and by some miracle sent you more in the direction of own life's purpose in order to fulfill your spiritual promise.

You and I, and everyone here on earth, has come into this world attempting to fulfill that promise. When we were born in this world we sacrificed a spiritual world. When we were born here we entered into a condition called sacrifice.

We all know what happens when we get here. It does not go the way you want it to.

So—therefore, we say it is not perfect. But, as a matter of scientific truth, everything here is perfect. We just don't like the way it is. So the problem is not what is here. The problem is our attitude toward it.

When the student is ready the teacher will appear.

A few years ago, through my own mistake and stupidity and an offer for a business venture in the Middle East, I lost everything that was precious to me; my home, my belongings and my business.

Down on my luck and no place to go to, I began to wonder around searching for myself and for the meaning of own life and some answers to make my life bearable. I spent much time in local parks and in public libraries because they were *free* and warm.

So—day by day, I began to find myself sinking deeper and deeper into depression. I was totally broke, financially, emotionally and especially *spiritually.* I began to blame God (as we often do) when we are down on our luck) for our misfortune. I started to look for the answers in other non-Muslim spiritual paths:

Hoping to find the royal road to riches and fortune I joined secret fraternal and spiritual organizations. Over the many years, I did Google search and found many spiritual paths that claimed to have found the only true path toward God.

I also joined some of those "Spiritual Organizations" to learn the truth first had. The funny thing is that every one of those Spiritual centers had a part of the real path toward God and it was right front of me but, I just didn't see it.

I guess, I was just looking for some tangible thing I could verify with five physical senses. I was trying to see the truth with my physical eyes. But, Spirit isn't physical and the human mind (Satan) will go against me in my Spirit.

Spiritual teachings I joined to find the Path toward God!

While dong Google search, I found a spiritual organization in Temecula California called *A Course in Miracles Foundation* (ACIM) Late Dr. Kenneth Wapnick was the director of that Christian base foundation. I attended his introductory seminar in Temecula, California. I was truly drawn to this highly spiritual man.

A Course in Miracles book consists of a 'self-study; **thought-system.** As a three volume curriculum consisting of a **Text, Workbook for students, and Manual for teachers.** I became a favorite student of Dr. Kenneth Wapnick.

In order to express *my* own thoughts on *A Course in Miracles* and my own journey with the Course based on my thirty-five years of real-life, extensive and practical experience in applying such ideas, I self-published a book under the title: **The Original Sin** as a joint venture with Dr. Kenneth Wapnick. (Available at www.amazon.com).

Turning points

Life is a series of turning points. Retrace some early turning points in your own life, and you will realized that they occurred at a crucial moment and is an eloquent tribute to the hands of God in your own life, as it did mine.

As Allah is my witness, an invisible force took control of events and by some miracle sent me in the direction of my next turning point in my own life. As I recall, that my wife and I had just returned from the **UMRA** (the pilgrimage of the Mecca), and package was waiting for me in the mail.

This package was from an organization known as the – "The Path of Spiritual Freedom." It is a new religious movement founded by a man named **PAUL TWITCHELL.** The spiritual home is the temple of ECK in Chanhassen, Minnesota.

In order to become aware of the teachings of this modern-day religion, I became a paid member. Received the second initiation into this path after two years of self-study discourses. I became the ECK **ARAHATA** (requirements of becoming a teacher of the Path of Spiritual Freedom organization).

The holy book of the teachings of this spiritual path was the two-volumes **The Shariyat- ki- Sugmad.** (Paul Twitchell, the modern-day founder of the Path of Freedom chose the word SUGMAD for God or Allah).

Being a full time student of this teachings taught me knowledge of the creation by Allah. Anyone who has been a student of the **NAHJUL BALAGHA by Imam Ali ibn Abu Talib, and** is aware of his Sermons for any length of time knows that divine creation is split into two parts; the lower and the higher planes.

The Spiritual Planes of God.

The lower planes are a material realm of time, matter, space, and energy—and the physical plane, of course, belong here. It is a training ground for self-realization.

The higher planes, your spiritual goal whether you know it or not, are that area beyond time and space; *the true worlds of God. This is a training ground for God-realization.* (Please understand my intent isn't to prove the existence of these lower and higher planes because modern libraries are full of books on the subject.)

Interestingly enough, my inner and our teaching of both the *A Course in Miracles* and this Path of Freedom came together to mold and shape a whole new spiritual consciousness; *a door to the magnificent Allah's worlds inside of me.* **They are the true gateway to heaven.** Frankly, there were many such episodes in my own life. Often too minor to stand out at the time, they nevertheless proved to be major turning points. For example, due to some personal reasons and a major turning point, I decided to leave the organization. (I'll talk more about this later).

But, you know what?, Still, the great truth kept just a jump ahead of me. So you can imagine the distress, the frustration, and the agony I was going through not being able to find the true path toward God.

Suddenly, I was intuitively guided to another spiritual path: the *Movement of Spiritual Inner Awareness.* (MSIA). It's a non-denominational, ecumenical (Christian base) church, incorporated in the State of California as a non-profit organization, based in Los Angeles.

The purpose is to teach Soul Transcendence, which is becoming aware of yourself as a Soul and as a one with Allah, *not* as a theory but, a living reality in daily life. This movement was begun by a man names **John-Roger** who held the keys to the 'Mystical-Traveler' Consciousness.(Soul Transcendence is taught by MSIA).

So—to make the long story short, I became a full time student of the *MSIA* teachings and became a seminar leader of the **Soul Awareness Seminars,** a gatherings that offers a direct and intimate inner experience the Soul Awareness within us, using a recorded message of the founder **John-Roger** or the current spiritual director and the Mystical Traveler—**John Morton.**

As Allah is my witness, most of own adult life, I have sensed myself as if there is a part of me that is **non-physical**, and loves me and longs to communicate with me. I didn't understand it. I thought I was going crazy. So, I didn't tell anyone.

I mean how do tell people, I see you as if on a motion picture screen and not associated with me. **I felt as if the whole world was an illusion or a dream.**

I made perfect sense to others, held very intelligent conversations but, to me it was as if someone else (Spirit) within me was holding the conversation.

The funny thing is that *The joy of alignment with the Spirit will flow over into EVERYTHING I did—including the most mundane aspects of my day-to-day life.* Somehow all my worldly needs were met as if someone was protecting me.

*****

And—then came the NAHJUL BALAGA.

I WAS TRULY INTRIGUED BY THE SELECTIONS FROM THE WRITING OF OUR MASTER AMIR AL-MU'MNIN,'ALI IBN ABI TALIB AND HIS LETTERS TO THE ENEMIES, AND THE GOVERNMORS OF THE PROVENS, INCLUDING SELECTIONS OF HIS LETTERS OF APPOINTMENT TO HIS ADMINSTRATIVE OFFICERS, AND HIS INJUNCTIONS TO MEMBERS OF HIS FAMILY AND HIS COMPANIONS.

New book is born....

The most interesting thing (at least to me anyway) about this Allah's intervention in my own deep search for the meaning of life is, that slowly but surely, some of these Sermons, Letters and Sayings of Imam Ali inb Abu Talifs had the most impact than others on my mind—thus the birth if his new book.

I remember, during my high school days, living in Sialkot City, in Pakistan, most of my close friends were non-Shia (Sunis) Muslims. And, they otfen asked me why do Shias Muslims believe that Imam Ali ibn Abu Talib should have been the very first **Khalifa,** after the Prophet's death?

I used to tell them, suppose I was the owner of several big fast food restaurants chain (say McDonalds) and would I leave them to my own 'kin-folks' or to just friend-folks after my death?

They had no clue as to what in the heck I was talking about, so they will inevitably say: *Of course, to your our 'kin-folk' or family.* What a dumb question? Then, I would say: **"Exactly, that's why the Khalifat of Islam should have gone to Imam Ali ibn Abu Talib.".** He was the kin and the family member of the Prophet. Imam Ali was the cousin and the son-in-law of the Prophet. How close can you be?

Lest I be misunderstood I wish here to state most emphatically that it is not my intent to prove who should be the first **Khalifa or the successor** (leader of the Caliphate), but I feel entitled to suggest that as true Muslim, perhaps we should try to look 'outside' the box (so to speak), for the true answers.

Just observe the slow evolution of human race. Sure, we have advanced enormously technologically, but as a race we are still doing the same destructive things that were reported in the Bible thousands of years ago.

Sure enough, this book **NAHJUL BALAGHA**, began to give me the answers. For example, my adversity due to a failure in a business venture in the Middle East lasted just over a year—but, Imam Ali ibn Abu Talib's adversity due to the loss of the God-given right and the privilege of being the very first **Khalifa of the religion Islam after the death of the Prophet** (p.b.u.h) lasted **more than twenty five years.** Just think of it!

Twenty-five years, living in that adversity, among those three "non-deserving" Khilafas one after another, for 25 long years, is an experience not calculated to give one sustained hope, I assure you, but Imam Ali ibn Abu Talik, knew right from the beginning to sacrifice and pay the price in time and education people to save the religion of Islam. *I believe sometimes you have control by giving control.*

Imam Ali ibn Abu Talib knew very well that *every adversity, every failure and every heartache carries with it the 'Seed' of an equivalent or a greater Benefit.* So when the seed of that opportunity was germinated after more than twenty-five years, people asked him to become the fourth Khilafa of the religion of Islam.

The funny thing is that even as a Shia Muslim, I knew all about Imam Ali ibn Abu Talib. We all that Imam Ali should have been the very first **Khalifa** of the Prophet Muhammad(p.b.u.h), but we never ever read the **NAHJUL BALAGHA**.

---

as-Sayed Mohamed Askary Jafery says: "This book contains such examples of chaste language, noble eloquence and super wisdom that non but ALI can produce such a work … He was the greatest source of wisdom of the religion preached by the Holy Prophet (AS.) This famous book NAHJUL BALAGA is the work which makes one realize the Great Mind of Ali ibn Abu Talib. NO BOOK CAN SURPASS IT BUT, the HOLY QUR'AN.

Writer's Limitations

"A writer or a speaker can only express his thoughts about a mortal like himself, but the Holy Qur'an is the words of the Supreme Being.

It is said, that reading the holy Qur'an, reflecting upon the meaning of its verses and practicing what the holy Qur'an preaches all are virtuous deeds.

It simply is not possible to convey in full the meaning of the verses of the holy Qur'an.

All the translations of the holy Qur'an, have fallen far behind the linguistic beauty of the original as well as it's ideas.

The English translation of a few select verses of the holy Qur'an are meant only to be a ground work for this unique book **NAHJUL BALAGHA** implications of the holy verses."

MUSHTAQ HAIDER JAAFRI

**The Holy Qur'an
is the full text
of divine guidance
for Man-Kind.**

**Surely, in Our hands is guidance ...
And to Us belongs the hereafter...
And the worldly life.** (Al-Layl 92:2)
----THE HOLY QUR'AN -----

*****

THE STORY OF THE SERPENT
The Holy Qur'an – Chapter Two, AL-BAQARA –
(S.V. Mir Ahmad Ali)

"And said We "O" Adam dwell thou and thy mate in the Garden of Eden and eat ye two therefrom freely as ye two wish and approach not ye this tree lest ye two will be the transgressors!"

"What that means in plain language is that God said to Adam and Eve that both of them live in the Garden of Eden and should eat freely all fruits of the Garden of Eden."

"But He (God) warned them against the fruit of this forbidden tree, and if they did, then, they should surely die.'

"The whole point I'm trying to convey here is that Allah made two things perfectly clear to Adam and Eve. First, they should never eat the fruit of the forbidden tree."

"Second, they were to remember that Satan is truly their enemy and will always go against their spiritual pursuits and Satan will always win because of his selfish and cunning nature."

"Allah made it abundantly clear to both Adam and Eve that that everything else in the Garden of Eden was there just for their own use as their desired,"

Speaking for myself, I sometimes imagine how human life must have been if Adam and Eve had not eaten the fruit of the forbidden tree.

In the beginning, there were only Allah and his creations. Only Adam and Eve were the Allah's creations that were made quite superior to all of His other creations. It was a happy family.

By listening to all the Satan's lies, at some strange moment, Adam and Eve believed that they could separate themselves from their own Creator.

"The fact that we are all here on the planet earth and not in Heaven would seem to indicate that the separation (between God and Adam and Eve(the parent's of the human race) did occur."

In our own way of thinking, it did seem to happen. In other words, Adam and Eve saw themselves as having a *will* that is separate from God and they both chose something different than what had chosen for them.

The sad this, however; is that this deliberate 'act' showed a power of choice—thus, the birth of the human ego within us which became a tool for Satan to use in order to manipulate human conscious to do what he (Satan) want them to do.

I believe from the bottom of my heart that you'll find that this Book: **NAHJUL BALAGAH,** actually deals with the *correction- process* of human perception of separation from

Allah and **none—but—Hazarat Iman Ali ibn Abu Talib can produce such a master piece book to show the way.**

So—the story goes, that Adam and Eve began to live a pleasant, peaceful, carefree life in the garden of Eden in Haven.

They played wherever they pleased. They slept whenever they pleased. They ate whatever their heart desired In a way, both were having a wonderful, great time enjoying the fruits of the Garden of Eden in Heaven.

I sometimes imagine that being humans, every time Adam and Eve came near the forbidden tree, they must have wondered. **"Why Allah did had told us to never go near hat tree?**

*I mean, what made that particular tree different from all others? Day by day they must have become more and more **curious** about the tree, but since they were warned against eating the fruit, they never dared to try.*

I also believe that perhaps, the mental state of 'curiosity' came into the human psyche when Adam and Eve became extremely curious about the forbidden tree in the Garden of Eden in Heaven.

For example, if I asked you at this very moment: **"Don't think of the pink elephant?'** Chance are that you are thinking of the pink elephant, because its human nature to become curious.

No one had ever become curious about anything before. Whatever God said, it was done, no questions asked. Obeying God's will was always priority number one—until, God gave human beings the 'power-of choice' to do as they will.

Meanwhile, Satan was dispelled from the Garden of Eden from Heaven. All the doors to heaven were shut tightly for Satan. There was no way possible for Satan that he could enter the Garden of Eden.

So there was no way possible that Satan could beguile Adam and Eve from Heaven But, Satan was busily engaged in trying to find ways and means to put his "third-wish' in motion.

I have said this many times before but, I think it's worth repeating again that Satan was the master of disguise and a very cunning.

Satan could influence others by trickery and by flattery and could mislead anyone in hundred different ways.

Satan finds a way

Satan finally found a serpent (a huge snake) outside the Garden of Eden that had an easy access to the doors of the Garden in Paradise in Heaven. Satan became a dear friend of this Serpent and won the serpent's heart by flattery.

"How fortunate the Serpent was to be able to visit the Garden of Eden in Paradise in Heaven whenever it wanted; Satan said.

"And, he (Satan) told the serpent sad stories about how much he missed all of his friends in the Garden of Eden and how wonderful it would be if he could just visit them even just for a short time."

Satan pleaded for help and told the serpent the he especially wanted to see Adam and Eve and to let them know how sorry he was for disobeying God's command.

The serpent, of course, knew nothing about what Satan was up to with his sad stories and flattery.

The serpent only knew that Satan was dispelled and thrown out of the Garden of Eden with humiliations.

And, the serpent knew that Allah was outraged with Satan for not obeying His command to prostrate before Adam therefore; Satan was prohibited from entering into the Garden of Eden where Adam and Eve lived.

"How fortunate the serpent was to be able to visit the Garden of Eden in Heaven whenever it wanted; Satan said to the serpent in a humble voice.?

Satan began to tell the serpent sad stories about how much he missed all of friends in the Garden of Eden and how wonderful it would be if only he could visit them—even just for a few moments.

Satan pleaded Serpent for help and told the serpent over and over again that he especially wanted to see Adam and Eve

to let them know how sorry he was for disobeying Allah's command.

The serpent, of course; knew nothing about what the Satan was up to and why he was so determined to visit Adam and Eve in Heaven.

The sad thing is that the serpent began to feel sorry for Satan by listening to his pleas and almost begging for a chance to enter the Garden of Eden to visit his friends. (I believe the act of begging came into being by the Satan).

The serpent began to think that there was no real harm in helping Satan enter in the Garden of Eden., but didn't know just how it can be possible without anyone knowing about it.

That is where the Satan's cunning third wish played a major role. As you recall, with that third wish Satan was given the power to enter into any physical body and communicate with others through the human mind.

Serpent did agree to let Satan use his body as a mean to transport Satan in the Garden of Eden. A date and time was set when Satan would enter the serpent's mouth into his body and talk to others.

Serpent was extremely pleased for deceiving the serpent and being able to enter the Garden of Eden and accomplish his two goals. The very first goal was to beguile Adam and Eve from Heaven and take his revenge.

The second goal was to become a major instrument for causing pain and suffering in every human life, from the moment of their birth, through the end of life, which is death.

Satan's third and final wish, as you recall was intended to do just that by entering in minds of every human being that ever lived on the surface of the earth and turning every human being against God.

As a footnote, I just want to say that it was quite interesting to note (at least to me anyway) that, Satan was created of the evolution of fire, but Adam was created by Allah Himself.

Because of Satan's many years of love and devotion and worships to God, Satan was allowed to stay in the Garden of Eden with other angels who were created of Spirit and mingle with them.

That is why, perhaps, Satan was reluctant to prostate before Adam in front of all the angels in the Garden of Eden, and refused to obey Allah's command.

But, by way of his third wish, Allah changed Satan into an unseen spirit. Satan's this 'act' of refusal to obey Allah was his PRIDE.

The sad thing is that before Satan was driven away from the Garden of Eden, Satan stood boldly in front of all the angels and said: by way of the power to enter any human mind, he will influence the human race to go against God.

In a way, Satan challenged God by proudly shouting that he will come upon them from the right side t and from the left side to steer them toward the wrong path away from God.

The Holy Qur'an – Chapter VII, AL-A'RAF
(S.V. Mir Ahmad Ali)

Said he:" As thou hast deprived me, surely will I lay wait for them in The straight (right) *path. Then, I will surely come upon them in from before them, and from behind them and from their right side and from their left side: and thou wilt not find more of them thankful."*

This was a Satan's challenge and promise to God.

What that means in plain language is that Satan said to Allah that since he (Satan) had been deprived of his rightful place in Heaven, Satan, would be waiting for them (human race) in their rightful path to misguide them in every wy possible.

Satan said that he would always attempt to mislead them in every way possible. He (Satan) would come upon them from the right side and from the left side and from up and down until they all come under his spell and do whatever I instruct them to do.

Satan said: "*Surely, I will endeavor to do my level best to create among them the perception of separation from God by every means possible—and God would not find more human beings thankful to Him.*" (This was the promised of Satan).

Hearing these Satan's words, Allah said to Satan: "Remember this Always, that no one who truly loves Allah can ever go astray by your influence or deeds. Allah said that only those people who believe in the satanic acts and did not believe in the straight (right) path would follow Satan as their friend or guardian." (This was the Promise of God to Satan).

You know, as I look back at the history of mankind, there is a clear evidence that Satan did seem to win with most of the human race but, he could never ever influence those people who loved God the most.

For example, when Allah asked prophet Abraham to slaughter and sacrifice his one and only son *Issaac, on Mount Moriah,* Satan went to his wife **Haj'rah, and told her to stop her husband from performing this vicious and cruel act of slaughtering her only son.**

It is a fact that **Haj'rah** immediately started to throw stones at Satan and yelling, **"Satan be gone" for my husband has received the command from Allah to sacrifice his son.** (Such is the power of the belief in Allah's commands).

Allah loved Haj'rah's act of throwing the stones at Satan so much that this particular act became a mandatory ritual to perform during the Muslim's most holy Day of **Huj** in the holy city Mecca.

The sacredness of this act of throwing the stones at Satan is, that the ceremony of the holy **Huj** isn't considered complete until all of the million's Muslims perform this symbolic act to throwing stones at Satan during the ceremony of the Huj.

The point I am trying to convey here is that Allah also promised Satan that people who love Allah the most will *never* be influenced by Satan's deceptive schemes no matter what they had to sacrificed for it.

My Christian friends and associates in America tell me that the crucifixion of the Jesus Christ was the ultimate evidence of the power of Satan to try to influence even the holy messengers of Allah and holy prophets and Imams.

It is said: that while on the cross, with nails pushed through his hands and feet, Jesus Christ was heard several times saying:

"Be gone Satan." "Be Gone Satan."

Apparently as if Jesus Christ seeing Satan and yelling loudly at Satan."

Later, Jesus was also heard repeating: *"Forgive them, O' Lord for they know not."* Such is un-shakable power and the strength of Holy people who Love Allah.

As I look back to the history of mankind especially, to the Muslim history, I have noticed with profound interest that Satan could never shake people who loved Allah the most. (As Shia Muslims, we are all aware of the story of Karbla).

The Story of Karbla

For example, most recently, Imam Hussain, the grandson of the Prophet Mohammed (p.b.u.h) was slaughtered after refusing to give him any water or food and letting him starve for three days in the scorching heat of the sand in the desert of karbla. His head was cut from his neck and the army of horsemen walked over his dead body. Just think of it!

As if it wasn't enough, that Imam Hussain's head was cut-off from his body an all those merciless people killed his only six months old infant son **Ali Asghar** was killed with an arrow piercing this little infant's throat.

To top this inhuman act, when Imam Husain buried his six months old infant son in the ground, these merciless people, dug the grave, pulled the six months child and cut his head also and put it on an arrow raising high to be displayed to other people in the crowd cheering the victory. Just imagine that!

The point I am trying so hard to convey here is that these people loved Allah the most and were willing and ready to sacrifice anything and everything even life itself **but will never bowed down to the satanic demands of Satan's army of Allah forsaken, misguided people.**

SELECTIONS FROM THE LETTERS AND PREACHINGS OF IMAM ALI IBN ABU TALIB, INCLUDING HIS REPLIES TO QUESTIONS AND MAXIMS MADE FOR VARIOUS PURPOSES. Excerpt from the book: NAHJUL BAKAGA by Imam Ali ibn Abu Talib

LETTER 77 – Given to 'Abdullah ibn al'Abbas, at the time of his being deputed to confront the Kharijities.

"Do not agure with them by the Qur'an because the Qur'an has many face. You would say your own and they would say their own; but argue with them by the *sunnah*, because they cannot find escape from it."

LETTER 78 – To Aba Musa al- Ash'arf in reply to his letter regarding the two arbitrators, Sa'id ibn Yahya al-Umawi has mentioned this in his "Kitab al-maghazi.

"Certainly, many people have turned away from many a (lasting) benefits (of the next life), for they bent towards the world and spoke with passions. I have been struck with wonder in this matter, upon which people who are self-conceited have agreed."

"I am providing a cure for their wounds but I fear lest it develops into a clot of blood (and becomes incurable)

Remember no person is more covetous than for the unity of the *ummah* of Muhammad (May Allah bless him and his descendants) and their solidarity. I seek through it good reward and an honorable place to return to."

"I shall fulfill what I have pledge upon myself even though you may go back from the sound position that existed when you left me last, because wretched is he who is denied the benefit of wisdom and experience."

"I feel enraged if anyone speaks wrong, or if I should worsen a matter which Allah (God)has kept sound. Therefore, leave out what you do not understand, because wicked people will be conveying to you vicious things; and that is the end of the matter."

*****

SELECTIONS FROM THE LETTERS AND PREACHINGS OF IMAM ALI IBN ABU TALIB, INCLUDING HIS REPLIES TO QUESTIONS AND MAXIMS MADE FOR VARIOUS PURPOSES.

Excerpt from the book: NAHJUL BAKAGA by Imam Ali ibn Abu Talib

LETTER 79 – To the army officers when Amir al- mu'minin became Caliph.

"Now, what ruined those before you was that they denied people their rights and then they had to purchased them (by bribes), and they led the people to wrong and they followed it."

*****

SERMON 69

Excerpt from the : NAHJUL BALAGHA
by Imam Ali ibn Abu Talib

SERMON 69– Spoken on the morning of the day When Amir al-mumnin was fatally Struck with sward.

"I was sitting when sleep came over me. I saw the Prophet of Allah appear before me and I said: *"O' Prophet of Allah! What crookedness and enmity I had to face from the people."* **The Prophet of Allah said:** *"Invoke* **(Allah)** *evil upon them."* **But I said:** *"Allah* **(God)** *may change them for me with better one and change me for them with a worse ones."*

As- Sayyid ar-Radi says: "al-awad" means crookedness and *"al-laddad" means enmity,* and this is the most eloquent expression.

THE SEPARATION OF ADAM AND EVE

The serpent allowed Satan to enter his mouth and transported him to the Garden of Eden in Heaven to speak to Adam and Eve. Upon arriving in the Garden of Eden, Satan saw Adam and Eve standing before the forbidden tree.

They were wondering why Allah had warned them against eating the fruit of that tree. They wondered why that tree's fruit was different from all of the other trees in the Garden. They wondered what would happen if they ate the fruit.

Because Allah had commanded them *not* to eat the fruit of the forbidden tree, they would not have *any thoughts* of ever eating it because they knew what happened to Satan when he disobey Allah's command.

So—Adam and Eve just walked away from the forbidden tree.

Satan could tell that both Adam and Eve were pondering on something, but didn't say anything.

As you recall, Satan was granted his third wish to be able to control human minds at any time and take over human thinking by whispering his suggestion and thoughts. So, he began to whisper his evil suggestions at Adam and Eve.

Interestingly enough, this was Satan's very first attempt to control human minds by controlling human thinking.

The point I'm trying to convey here is that this was Satan's first *deliberate* evil 'act' to control human thinking by whispering his own evil thoughts into the human minds and take the their thinking and suggest evil things to do that will take them away from the path toward God.

*****

The Holy Qur'an – Chapter VII, AL-A'RAF (S.V. Mir Ahmad Ali)

"Then, whispered Satan evil suggestions unto the two (Adam and Eve) *that he might display unto what hath been kept hidden from them of their shame," and said he:* "Forbade not ye your Lord from this tree save lest ye two become angels or lest ye may become immortals."

What that means in plain language is that Satan whispered onto Adam and Eve that the only reason God forbade them to eat the fruit of the forbidden tree was that once they tasted the fruit, it would make them intelligent and wise and give them all the knowledge of the universe.

"Eating the fruit of this tree of knowledge and wisdom, the Satan said would make them like angels and also give them the ever-lasting life."

Surprisingly enough, Adam and Eve heard these whispers in their heads (minds) and suddenly looked up to see just who was suggesting all these notions into their own mind. The only thing they saw was serpent talking to them.

Apparently, Satan was speaking to them through the serpent's mouth. So, Adam and Eve asked the serpent,

"Is this really true?"

They wanted to know that just by eating the fruit of the tree of the knowledge and wisdom, they would become like angels and live forever.

Hearing this from Adam and Eve, Satan immediately began to swear up and down. Satan said: *"I swear by the almighty God who created all of us, every word I say to you is true.*

It is said that Satan was the very first to utter Allah's name in in vain. Even the Holy Bible says: **Thou shalt not take the name of the Lord thy Allahin vain. And,** also… **"You shall not make wrongful use of the name of the Lord."** (The word Lord referred to Allah or Christian God).

This is one of the Ten Commandments. It is a prohibition of blasphemy, specifically, the misuse or "**taking** in vain" of the name of the God.

Satan was known to by very cunning and was the first to the to take the name of Allah in vain to *win* the trust of someone. Satan said:

"I swear by all mighty Allah that I am indeed your friend and not your enemy. **You can trust me and consider a sincere counselor."**

The Holy Qur'an – Chapter VII AL-A'RAF
(S.V. Mir Ahmad Ali)

"And, he (Satan) **swore unto them both:** *Verily unto you a sincere advisor."*

With these few words the serpent left the Garden of Eden and brought Satan down from Heaven.

As you can imagine, Satan surely has instigated many evil, untrue suggestions into the minds of the Adam and Eve.

Then, suddenly Eve said to Adam :

What could go wrong if we just taste a little bit of the fruit of the forbidden tree? **As the serpent said, it may bring us the knowledge of the universe and an ever-lasting life which we could enjoy here together forever.**

So—then, day by day, Eve really began to insist Adam that we should just try to taste the fruit and see for ourselves whether what Satan is telling us is true or false.

At first, Adam absolutely refused to listen to Eve's desire to eat the fruit of the forbidden tree, which Satan has been so successful in instigated in her mind by both the deceit and by swearing that he (Satan) was indeed their true friend and a sincere confidant.

The point I am trying so hard to make here about *not* eating the fruit of the forbidden tree is that Satan had instigated both of them by deceit so that they would be curious enough to at least try to taste the fruit of the forbidden tree.

Adam and Eve had absolutely no clue as to what to expect or what would take place within their own personality-structure.

The Holy Qur'an – Chapter VII AL-A'RAF
(S.V. Mir Ahmad Ali)

"Then, he instigated them both by deceit so when they tasted (of) the tree their shameful things got developed unto them, and they got displayed onto them, and they both began covering themselves with the leaves of the garden; and called out onto them their Lord (saying):

"Did I not forbid ye two that tree, and (did I not) say unto you both that Satan is of ye both a declared enemy."

Holy Bible and the Holy Qur'an

It's quite interesting to note, (at least to me anyway) what this verse of the Holy Qur'an Chapter VII Al-A'RAF says is somewhat the same as the Holy Bible Chapter II, GENESIS.

The Holy Qur'an says that once Adam and Eve did eat the fruit of the forbidden tree, their 'private-parts' began to develop and began to feel shameful about it.

In the Holy Bible, Chapter Genesis 2, which ends with Adam and Eve standing naked before each other without shame because they had not eaten the fruit as yet.

Shame is really another word for guilt—and shamelessness *is the expression of the pre-separation condition.* In other words, there was no guilt because there had been no sin. Sin is guilt, but not the ***original sin.***

It is the third chapter of Genesis that touches on the original sin, and that begins with Adam and eve eating the forbidden fruit. The act of doing that constituted their disobedience with God, and that really is the sin. What I am trying to convey here is this:

Satan knew very well that shame would bring guilt into Adam's and Eve's minds, and their desire for knowledge and everlasting life would create a *will* in them that is separate from Allah's Will.

And they *could* choose something different from what Allah had wanted for them. That again is the birth of ego: *the belief that sin is possible.*

The Holy Bible says: "So—they eat the forbidden fruit, and the very first thing they do after that is to look at each other – and this time they do feel shame and *cover* their private-parts.

They put fig leaves around their sexual organs and this becomes an expression of their guilt (just the way Satan had planned). They realized that they had done something sinful, and the nakedness of their bodies became the symbol of their sin.".

*****

Hearing the voice of God

"The very first thing that follows is that Adam and Eve hear the voice of Allah, Who is already looking for them, and they now become afraid of what Allah will do if He catches up with them.

So—they hide in the bushes so Allah will not find them."

"Right there you see an example of the belief in sin—that you can separate yourself from Allah – with the feeling of having done so, and then the fear of what will happen if Allah catches up with us and punishes us.

AND THEN CAME . . . NAHJUL BALAGHA

Sure enough, Allah catches up with them. Allah says to Adam and eve, "where have you been lately?" Adam and Eve replied, "We have been hiding in the bushes." Allah said: "Why?"

They said: "Because we are naked."

Allah said: "How do you know you are naked?"

They replied: "We can see our sexual organs and sense an instinct to mate." Allah said:

"How did it happen?" They said: *We did eat the fruit of the forbidden tree.*"

Allah said: **"Did I not forbid you both to never ever go near that tree and eat that forbidden tree?"**

Habit of Passing the Buck

Interestingly enough, here we see how human habit of "passing the buck" (so to speak) or blaming others for our own mistake came into human psyche. Adam blamed Eve and vice versa.

Adam said:

"I'm not the one to blame it was Eve who made me eat the fruit."

So—Allah looks at Eve and said:

"Woman, why did you make Adam eat that fruit?"

101

Eve replied,

"I am not the one to blame, it was serpent that said if we eat this fruit we will become like angels and become wise and live forever?"

*****

So—to make a long story short, Adam and Eve got down on their knees and asked Allah to forgive them for not only eating the fruit of the forbidden tree but, also following the command of the Satan to trust him, while Allah had made abundantly clear the Satan was their enemy.

Allah does not condemn anyone but, forgive. God's Love is nevertheless the basis of forgiveness. Allah said: *"they should get down on earth and It would provide them with substance for a fixed time.* Allah's voice speaks to you and me all through the day. It is hidden under the ego's (Satan) senseless thoughts which we have cluttered our minds.

Speaking for myself, what I've found is that any expression of our anger – whether it is in the form of a mild twinge of annoyance, or intense rage (it doesn't make any difference; they are all the same) – is always an attempt to justify the projection of our guilt or anger.

All fear comes from our belief that we should be punished for what we have done or not don. And we'll be afraid of what the punishment will be. Anger is nothing more than my own decision to project guilt onto someone else.

I guess I learned that from Adam and Eve, the parents of the human race. SELECTIONS FROM THE <u>SAYINGS</u> AND PREACHINGS OF IMAM ALI IBN ABU TALIB, INCLUDING HIS REPLIES TO QUESTIONS AND MAXIMS MADE FOR VARIOUS PURPOSES.

Excerpt from the book: NAHJUL BAKAGA by Imam Ali ibn Abu Talib

13. Amir al-mu'minin, peace be upon him, said: "When you get (only) small favors do not push them awa through lack of gratefulness."

14. Amir al-mu'minin, peace be upon him, said: "He who is abandoned by near ones is dear to remote ones."

15. Amir al-mu'minin, peace be upon him, said: "Every mischief monger cannot even be reported."

Amir al-mu'minin uttered the sentence when Sa'd ibn Arl Waqqas, Muhannad ibn Maslamah and 'Adbullah ibn 'Umar refused to support him against people in Jamal. He means to syay that these people are so against me that neither have my words an effects on then nor do I reproof, rebuke or correct them.

*****

SERMON 73

Excerpt from the: NAHJUL BALAGHA
by Imam Ali ibn Abu Talib

SERMON 73 – When Consultative Committee (or Shura) decided to swear alliance to 'Uthman, Amir al-mu'mnin said:

"You have certainly known that I am the most rightful of all others for the Caliphate. By Allah so long the affairs of Muslims remain intact and there is no oppression in it save on myself I shall be keeping aloof from its attractions and allurements for which you aspire."

Sometimes it's necessary to have control over affairs by *giving* control to others. Although; Consultative Committee gave control to "Uthman, nevertheless the history proves that Inman Ali ibn Abu Talib had full and complete control of the **Challifate of the three Khalifas on the time until Imam Ali became fourth one.**

The point I'm trying to convey here is that Imam Ali ibn Abu Talib had full and complete control over the Islam affairs.

The group of people who followed the Imam Ali began to be known as the **Shia Muslims.**

Lest, I be misunderstood, I wish here to state most emphatically that it is not my intent to discuss whether Imam Ali ibn Abu Talib should have been the very first Calipha after the death of the Prophet Muhammad (p.b.u.h) or not, because modern libraries are full of books on the subject.

But I do feel entitled to suggest that the **Shia Muslims** simply means the followers of Imam Ali ibn Abu Talib after the death of the Prophet Muhammad (p.br.u.h.).

And, I consider myself to be a fortunate enough to be the follower of the Imam Ali ibn Abu Talib. One of the most often asked question is: **"Who are the Shia Muslims?** The best answer to this question was given by Sayed Mustafa Al-Qazamini, which I like to share with you next.

*****

(A Talk Given – **by Sayed Mustafa Al- Qazamini**)

WHO ARE THE SHIA MUSLIMS?

"Shia refers to a group of followers and Shia means followers and this term has been mentioned in the Holy Qur'an several times in reference to the followers of Abraham, and the Prophet Moses both and also in reference to Prophet Noha, Shia means the followers."

"Shias are those who follow the teachings of the Holy Qur'an and follow the traditions of the Prophet Muhammad (p.b.u. h).

Actually the first time the term Shia mentioned in Islam, it was by the Prophet Himself (p.b.u.h) when he revealed to Ali and his friends as being his followers.

In the Parable of Ali, Prophet Muhammed (p.b.u.h) **Says:**

"I am the root, Ali is the branch, Husan and Hussain are the fruit and Shias are the leaves."

Another tradition from the Prophet Muhammed (p.b.u.h) regarding the Shias, he said when he saw Ali coming: *YA –ALI* (referring to him) **this man (Ali) and his followers will indeed be the successful ones in the Day of Judgment."**

So—the Prophet was the first one to mention the term of Shias. In fact, to invent and come up in his lifetime when he

referred to Iman Ali and his followers in many occasions in different places.

The key to remember is this: Shias choose to follow the **AH LUL-BAT** (the immediate family of the Prophet) because these are the instructions of the Holy Qur'an and these are the instructions of the Prophet Muhammad (p.b.u.h). He said:

"*After my departure* (death) *I leave two things* Prophet Muhammad reminded Muslims on many occasions that after his death I leave behind among you two things.

First, the book of God the Holy Qur'an. Second my Ah-Lul-Bat – (including only **Ali, Fatimah, Hussan, Hussain and the Imams).**"

So, basically, Shias are the ones who follow **the Holy Qur'an, the Prophet** (p.b.u.h) and the family of the Prophet.

Iman BAKAR (the fifth Imam) *has another way of defining the Shias morally—and ethically and spiritually.* Speaking of moral and ethic and spiritual definition of Shias, Imam Bakar speaking to one of his companion said:

"YA - Jaffar, it's not enough for a person to call himself Shia, and then expect complete salvation and the success on the day of judgment."

In fact, the shia's of the prophet and his household are ones, who are pious, fear God they obey God, you'll recognize them by only humility then submission to God then honesty.

Their abundance praise of God, then fasting, their prayers, their goodness to their parents, attention to the poor, needy, orphans.

They speak the truth, recite the Holy Qur'an, holding back their tongues *expect for good words—and trust worthy of other religions and to all people.*

These are characteristics of the Shia Muslims. Shias, who follow God, the Holly Qur'an, the Prophet Muhammad, and after him the nearest people of Prophet who have been appointed by God and his prophct and those are the **AH-LUL-BAT,** the family of the Prophet.

Also they have good qualities, in their behaviors and attitudes and conduct themselves the way to reach out to others.

They are excellent, they are the tough ones and the followers of the Muhammad and **the manners of treating people with kindness.**

Shia Muslims follow Imam Ali and Bee Bee Fatima and her Family members Imam Hussan, Imam Hussain and Imam Jaffar saddique and other Imams.Those Shias who are the followers of the Imam Jaffar Sadque's teachings are called the **Jaafries.**

I'm one of those Shias who are the followers of the imam Jaffar Saqique's teaching and I am Mushtaq Haider Jaafri, attempting to share my story ith you.

How I became a Shia Muslim?

Speaking for myself, I have 'duel-religions' family. What I mean is that from my mother side we were all non-Shia religion family. From my father side we were all Shia-religion family. Believe you me that it was pretty tough to keep harmony and peaceful relationship between the two-sides of the religion.

When I visited my mother's side of the family of course; they wanted me to join their way of religious thinking. They didn't believe that the Prophet Mohammad (p.b.u.h) was the last Prophet on Earth and had their own prophet and holy places for worships.

The amazing thing is that they had the very same Holy Qur-an of the Prophet (p.b.u.h), and worshiped the same God and performed the same five-prayers daily, even prayed the same way.

They only believed that the Prohet Muhammad (p.b.u.h) wasn't the last Prophet on the surface of the earth. One big difference between my mother and father sides of the Muslim religion was that my mother side religion didn't think that the sacrifice of the grandson of the Prophet Muhammad **Imam Husain** (the third Imam) to **save Islam,** was so special or sacred or spiritual ritual to celebrate through the streets of city in order to keep it alive.

My mother side of Muslim religion was totally against *beating chesst* (**matan-ah Husain**) and the annual rituals of Majlises (meetings) during the first ten days of the (Arabic) month of the Muharam. (Arabic calendar has only 28 days in a month following moon every 14 days of the month.) When I was a young boy, living with my parents in Sialkot City, Pakistan, **Moulana Hafiz Kafait Husian,** *was a very prominent Shia Scholar and 'Hafaza Quran'* (memorized the whole Qur'an) *and well respected 'Alam'* (Prominent religious leader) *in the Shia-religion teachings of ISLAM.*

He (Moulana Hafiz Kafiat Husain) **displayed all the characteristics and the qualities of the people of the followers of Imam Ali ibn Abu Talib (as described in the talk of the Syed Mustafa Al-Qazamini)**

One thing I vividly remember that Moulana Hafiz Kafait Husain is that during the first ten days of Muharam (First month of the Arabic Calendar) , he would come to our home in Sialkot, City, Pakistan for performing the ten majlises in our Imam-Bar-Ghah and that he would always stay with us in our home.

He would explain the story of Karbala. He would explain to my father, my mother and all Uncles who are the Shia Muslims, the followers of the Imam Ali ibn Abu Talib and the rest of the Imams.

Sure enough, Lo and Behold, he told us we are the follower of the teachings of Imam Jaffar Sadique (the sixth Imam) and my parents, from the father side and my Uncle first convert to the Shia Muslim religion.

We added our last name Jaafri to show our alliance to Imam Ali and the other Immans. From my mother side only her accepted the Shia Muslim religion. (Perhaps, for the reason, her name is **Zainib**).

My parents became devoted to the Shia religion. Every Muharam, my father would leave all worldly duties and spend the ten days in the sadness of Imam Husain, helped prepare the ZULJINAH (decorate the Imam Husain's horse) on the tenth day of the ASHURA (Mohram).

My own mother on the other hand, became a teacher and participating in the ladies- majlises telling the story of the sacrifice of Imam Husain with his family including the six month of baby son Ali **Asghar** died with an arrow in his throat.

Iman Zain-UL-Abideen (the fourth Imam) was with his father Imam Husain in Karbla during fight between good and evil.

He saw everything with his own eyes how the cruel and merciless army of more than ten thousands trained fighter cut Imam Husain's head and ran horses over his body in the scorching heat of the Arabian desert.

Imam Zain – UL – Abideen saw their tents burned in blazing red hot flames. He saw how the army displayed the heads of his family and companions on the arrows and marched through the streets to disgrace the family of the Prophet and the followers of Imam Ali ibn Abu Talib.

The army showed whatever was against the true teachings of the Prophet of the religion of Islam.

The point I am trying to convey here is that Imam Zain UL – Abideen emphasized throughout his life to ***never ever*** forget the story of Karbla and let the sacrifice of the lives of the seventy-two companion along with Imam Husain die or vanish on the surface of the world.

It is said that Iman Zain –UL – Abdeen cried throughout his life in the remembering the humiliation and disgrace of his family. Imam himself was too week, extremely sick to even walk, otherwise he would have been slaughtered.

It's quite amazing (to me anyway) that if you are the Shia Muslim and true follower of the Imam Ali ibn Abu Talib, you cannot (and I mean cannot) stay at home and not to go to Imam – Bar – Gah and listen to the full story of Karbla.

I don't care how tired you are or how old you are, you'll be there sitting among other lover of Iman Husain, crying their hearts out while the Moulans (Preacher of Majlis) tell the true story about most unhumane story of Karbla.

There is something magical about the story of Karbla. If you are a Shia Muslim, I'll bet you cannot stay home. I guarantee it. That's what makes us Shia Muslims and apart of from all other religions. I've seen many religious,and spiritual **movements come and go but not this movement.**

*****

Significance of the first ten days of Muhram

My father, Mr. Nazir Ahmad Jaafri was one of the Shia Muslins in our family. He was truly devoted follower of Imam Ali ibn Abu Talib.

One thing I remember the most about my dear father is that during *the first ten days of Muhran*, he would always take a leave of absence from his work no matter what.

And, if his employer did not grant the first ten days leave of absence from his work, he would quit work on the spot. The funny thing is that interestingly enough another job opening will be waiting for him right after the **ASHURA,** (the tenth day of Muhram).

No matter what city or how far he was working, my father would come to Sialkot city, Pakistan which was our home city. Immediately, he would go to the **Imam Bar-Gaha** (place to hold Muhram ten Majlises) and start to built the tent, set-up the loud-speaker system for the speakers so audience could hear far away and our main speaker was of course, **Moulana Hafiz Kafiat Husain** would come from Lahore and stay with us for ten days.

In all honesty, let me say this that I was too young to know the full significance of the Muhram.

Another thing I remember the most about my dear father is that in the day of the **ASHURA,** (the tenth day of Muhram), he would decorate the **ZULJINAH** (decorate the horse) with fancy covers and sword and red color to show a symbolic way in which Imam Hussain went to the battle field of Karbla and was slaughtered after being without food and water for three full days, along with his other family members and even his just six months old baby son **Ali Asghar.**

I was too young to know what was all this about but, I even cried my heart out, beat my chest along with other Shia doing **matam** (beating chest in sadness of Imam Husain).

Speaking for myself, I often felt an *inner* urge and a deep attachment to the story of Karbla. I often wondered that what is this thing inside of me that always compels me to hold sacred these ten days of the Muhram. My lifestyle always changed during these ten days of the Muhram.

I wondered that what is it that thing within me that keeps me want to keep the story of Karbla alive forever.

Surprisingly, every Muhran, I hear the same story verbatim, but it feels as if it happened yesterday.

Once an American friend of mine who is an excellent, successful 'human-rights' attorney by profession went to attend one these Majlis in our **Imam-Bar-Gah**, in Downey California where we lived.

He saw how **Moulana** (spiritual speaker) was sadly narrating the story of the Karbla, and how people, young and old, men and women and children were crying, beating their heads with their hands, as if someone in their family suffered recently a great tragedy of some sort. He was truly puzzled, and confused, to say the least.

The next day, my friend asked me to explain just what was going on there. I tried to explain to him how Imam Husain, the grandson of our Prophet Muhammad (p.b.u.h) was slaughter along with seventy two innocent people of his family and companions and even his six month son in Karbla due to a 'human-rights' issue in our religion.

I told him that Imam Husain (AS) was the grandson of the Prophet of Islam, and the **ruler of the Islam** (at the time) was a man who wasn't related to the Prophet and had no clue as to what the Islam should be. He demanded Imam Husain to swear an allegiance and support and commitment to him or die.

When Imam Hussain denied to his command, the ruler of the time challenged Imam Hussain to fight his vicious, cruel and inhumane army of more than 10,000 fully armed warriors. My attorney friend was truly saddened to hear the unfair challenge of the ruler of Islam.

The next day my attorney friend came to me and said Mr. Jaafri.

"I want to sue all those people who killed Imam Husain in Karbla?' But, when I told him that this incident did happen, more than fourteen hundred years ago, my attorney friend was astonished and said, **"you guys remember the Karbla incident as if it happened Just yesterday."**

Such is the power of this sacred sacrificed to save Islam from that ruler. My mother was the very first person who became Shia Muslim.

Her name was: **ZAINAIB.**

My own mother once told the story of Karbla and the importance of keeping this story alive until the day of judgment (Qamat), that I never ever forgot. I don't remember the exact words but I like to tell you in my own words.

The Story of Karbla as told by my mother.

My mother said that once our Prophet Muhammad (p.b.u.h) came to her daughter's home and while lying in the bed he asked her daughter Fatima that he was feeling a bit cold.

Fatima (AS) the beloved daughter of the Prophet gave her father a blanket to get warm and the Prophet fell asleep. Suddenly, Fatima (AS) noticed that her father was shivering in the bed and sweating as if seeing or hearing something very unpleasant or sad.

When the Prophet finally awoke, Bee Bee Fatima asked her beloved father about the reason of his trembling in the bed under the blanket she had given him to be warm. The Prophet told Fatima the full story of Karbla and how the ruler of the time will shame **Imam Husain**'s family member after keeping him without food and water and slaughtering him in pain and suffering.

Then, Fatima (AS) asked her father:

"No one will ever cry for my son Hussain and those 72 companions slaughtered with my son or sympathize and remember Imam Husain's story?'

Then, the Prophet **said: "Angle Gabrie**l has informed me that God will create a special group of people on the surface of the earth whose purpose in life would be to not only to cry and remember the story of Karbla but will keep the story of the sacrifice to save Islam from the unjust ruler of the time *alive* until the day of judgment to deal with them.

My mother used to proudly say:

"In a special way, God is keeping His promise with the Prophet (p.b.u.h) **of keeping the story of Karbla alive for mankind through the Shia Muslims."**

My mother used to tell me that Shia Muslims are chosen people from God to fulfill the promised of God with the Prophet Muhammad (p.b.u.h.). My mother would ask me to promise this to her.

My mother said that God made promised the Prophet that the young men and women of this group will cry for the young of the Karbla, and the old men and women and even all the children of this group will recite (sing) the sweat melodies to tell the story of Karbla.

What's more God will create the most learned men and women whose livelihood will depend on telling Imam Husain's story of Karbla and will perform their tasks with honor.

My mother said: *After hearing this story of Karbala from her father Prophet Muhmmad* (p.b.u.h) *Fatima* (AS) *promised to her father by saying that she* (Fatima) will not enter the gate of Heaven until all these men and women and children of this Shia group will enter Heaven ahead of her."

I sometime wonder that is why no one on earth could ever hurt this movement."

Since, the Imam Hussain's Karbla sacrifice to save Islam religion, millions have tried to stop this movement but, none has been successful because Allah had promised the loving daughter of the Prophet Mohammed (p.b.u.h) and they never will. I guarantee it!

*****

SELECTIONS FROM THE <u>SAYINGS</u> AND PREACHINGS OF IMAM ALI IBN ABU TALIB, INCLUDING HIS REPLIES TO QUESTIONS AND MAXIMS MADE FOR VARIOUS PURPOSES.

Excerpt from the book: NAHJUL BAKAGA by Imam Ali ibn Abu Talib

1. **Amir al-mu'minin, peace be upon him, said:** "During civil disturbing be like an adolescent camel who has neither a back strong enough for riding nor udders for milking."

> "*labun*" means a milch camal and "*ibnu.l labun*" means its two year old young. In this age the young is neither for riding nor does it has udders which could be milked. It is called "*ibnu'l labun*" because in this period of two years its its mother bears another young and begins yielding milk again. The intention is that during civil disturbance or trouble a man should behave in such a manner that he may be regarded of no consequence and ignored."

*****

A Foot Note to my story of KARBLA.

Moulana Hafiz Kafiat Husain became my "father-in-law'. When my wife and I came to America, there were not many Shia-Muslims. During the first Muharam we invited all Shia-Muslims we could find in the "Yellow-Pages" of the telephone book. (we found only 10 people). Then, we started holding the ten Majlises at our own homes and then at YWCA and at Christian rented Churches. Soon we began to grow in numbers. As of writing this book, there are five full-time Imam Bar-Bar Ghahs with more than three hundreds momneens (Shia-Muslims). Such is the power of the story of Karbla.

SERMON 28

Excerpt from the : NAHJUL BALAGAH
by Imam Ali ibn Abu Talib

SERMON – 28- About the transient nature of this world and importance of the next world.

"So now, surely this world has turned its back and announced its departure while the next world has appeared forward and proclaimed its approach."

"Today is the day of preparation while tomorrow is the day of race. The place to proceed to its Paradise while the place of doom is Hell. Is there no one to offer repentance over his faults before the day of trail?"

"Beware, surely you are in the days of hopes behind which stands death. Whoever acts during the days of his hope before approaching of his death, his action would benefit him and his death would not harm him. But, he who fails to act during the period of hope before the approach of death his action is a loss and his death is a harm to him."

"Beware, and act during the period of attraction just as you act during a period of dread.

Beware, surely I have not seen a coveter for Paradise asleep nor a dreader from Hell to be asleep?"

"Beaware, he whom right does not benefit must suffer the harm of the wrong, and he whom guidance does not keep firm will be led away by misguidance toward destruction."

"Beware, you have been ordered insistingly to march and have been guided how to provide for the journey."

"Surely the most frightening thing which I am afraid of about you is to follow desires and to widen the hopes."

"Provide for yourself from this world what would save you tomorrow (on the Day of Judgment)."

As-Sayyid ar-Radi says: "If there could be an utterance which would drag by neck towards renunciation in this world and force to action for the next world, it is this sermon.

It is enough to cut off from the entanglements of hopes and to ignite the flame of preaching (for virtue) and warning (against vice).His most wonderful words in sermon are *"Today is the day of preparation while tomorrow is the day of race.*

The place to proceed to is Paradise while the place of doom is Hell," because besides sublimity of words, greatness of meaning, true smiles and factual illustrations, there are wonderful secrets and delicate implications therein.

It is this saying that he place to proceed to is Paradise while the place to doom is Hell. Here he has used two different words to convey to convey two different meanings.

For Paradise he has used the word **"the place to proceed to" but for Hell this word has not been used.**

One proceeds to a place which he likes and desires and this can be true for Paradise. Hell does not have the attractiveness that it may be liked or proceeded to. We seek Allah's protection from it.

Since for Hell it was not proper to say "to be proceeded to" Amin al mu'minin employed the word **"doom"** implying the last place of stay where one reached even though it may mean grief and worry or happiness and pleasure.

This word is capable of conveying both senses. However, it should be taken in the sense of *"al-masir"* or *"al- ma'al"*, that is, last resort.

Qur'anic verse is

"say thou 'Enjoy ye (your pleasures yet a while) *for your last resort is unto the* (hell) *fire"* **(14:30).** Here to say *"sabqatakum"* that is, *"the place for you to proceed to"* in place of the word *"masirakum"* that is, your doom or last resort would not be proper in any way.

Think and ponder over it and see how wonderous is its inner implication and how far its depth goes with beauty. Amir al-mu'minin's utterance is generally on these lines. In some version the word *"sabqah"* is shown as *"subqah"* which is applied to reward fixed for the winner in race.

However, both the meanings are near each other, because a reward is not for an undesirable action but for good and commendable performance.

*****

Excerpt from a Local Radio Station

Not too long ago, I heard a story on a local radio—KYPA—in Hollywood, California. This radio station I was listening to had, at that time, a very highly motivational speaker who was telling a real-life incident.

He spoke about a medical doctor who worked in the hospital's emergency room (ER). This was the place where people were brought in after a fatal auto accident or a major heart attack.

All people brought into this particular hospital's emergency ward were usually in severe, critical condition, even to the point of near death experience.

I'm sure you probably have seen this on television in some of those hospital emergency-room shows where a person is brought in the operating room. He or she is then, hook-up to some EKG or EGG machine and, with the electrical electrodes, given a quick shock with the hope to retrieving the heart-beat and attempting to pour life into the body again.

On a television show, you see a doctor holding two discs, one in each hand, with wiring hooked-up to an oscilloscope where they could see the heart pulse.

Suddenly, the attending physician or doctor hits the two discs—*boom!—boom* and repeats aloud, one, two, three—*boom!*—again on the still unconscious person's chest, one on each side, and you see the person's body lying on the bed literally jerk up on the bed with each electrical shock as the disc hits the chest of the person.

If you have ever seen a medical TV show, then you'll know exactly what I'm talking about.

This is what this medical doctor did for living each and everyday, working in the emergency room, trying to put life back into the human body. Many times, the person would suddenly die, and he would verify their death by seeing a very straight line with a deep beep sound on the oscilloscope screen.

But then, once in a while, this doctor would witness that just a few minutes later, some of the human body would come back to life with no apparent medical or logical reasons or explanations, other than the doctor would notice that there would be a very loud pitch, or a "beep" on the screen of the oscilloscope with a definite pulse in the human body along with electrical peaks on the EKG or EGG machine showing the heart beating normally full speed again.

This medical doctor saw this miracle (so to speak) or this medical phenomenon in the operating room over and over again in the emergency ward of the hospital he worked at the moment. At first, he thought, that it was just a coincidence, and all those people who got their heart beats back and became alive again were those people who just happened to be lucky people who apparently, just got a second chance in life and got their life back.

But, this 'medical-pattern' happened too often to be just a coincidence. The doctor thought that it was indeed a miracle, to say the least, that the human body was dead for all practical, medical and logical reasons but, the Soul was still alive within the body.

The point I'm trying to convey her is that this particular doctor witnessed this miracle or the 'medical-pattern' in the emergency-room of that hospital he worked everyday just too many times to ignore this miracle or natures phenomenon, if you will. He wanted to get some answers to this riddle of life.

Then, one day, this medical doctor started his own private search and investigation to find some answers to this so-called life's miracle or phenomenon that, apparently, put life back in the human body, before his own eyes. This doctor become obsessed with this so-called miracle.

So—the doctor decided that the best way to find out the truth behind this 'entity' or the 'higher-energy' or Source or the universal-power within all of us that is biased in favor of life, that puts back life into the people he operated on, was to actually personally visit them, during his days off from work and during the holidays or weekends.

He decided to visit all those people he actually operated on in that hospital's emergency room and had died right in front of his own eyes—and did come back to life again. As the story goes, this doctor would visit all those people and ask each and every one of the very same questions: ***Tell me, what exactly happened during the time that you were a dead person?*** No one had every asked this question before, but this medical doctor wanted to know the real answer.

He visited as many people as he could find to ask this important question for his own private research, so that his findings could be documented in major medical journals for others to read the facts about what happens when we die? It is said that during the course of his own personal research and investigations to find the real answers, he visited over fifty people who had apparently died in his own emergency-room and did come back to life again.

He asked each of his patience the very same question: Tell me, what exactly happened during the time you were a dead person? And, how did you come back to life again? He asked this very same question to each of the fifty people he visited for his private investigation and research.

To his amazement, nearly everyone he visited, and asked the very same questions *gave* him identically the very same answer—verbatim! This is what this medical doctor documented in his report.

In essence, what all these patience said was that: *We literally saw ourselves coming out of our own bodies and suddenly we were in the air above you. We could see that you and your staff trying to start the heart beat.* There was no beep on the EKG or EGG machine just a straight line—indicating we were dead and you all gave up on us and left the operating room.

But, surprisingly, this was the beginning of a new phase of life for us. We all intuitively, became aware of ourselves as Soul—a divine part of Spirit—God. The essence of what we saw was a sense of being a spiritual beings and our inner vision opened up and saw a bright, beautiful, divine LIGHT, showing the worlds upon worlds.

A strange joy burst in our Souls. We heard a voice saying:

"We must now bear the duty of gathering up Souls for return to their true home in Heaven. We must act in loving with all beings, creation, world, and God.

With this short message we were returned into our physical bodies.*"The only thing that you can take with you—the only thing that is going to live, and never die—is the Soul."*

I imagine, just for a moment, that tomorrow is the last day of my life. What feelings does that thought inspire in my? One thing is for sure. From this moment on, I'll need to be **aware** of the possibility and the certainty of death, and come to terms with it.

This means, that most of the things I tend to focus energy on are going to begin to seem meaningless. As I focus on my death, I begin to focus on my priorities; on what is really important.

There is an old cliché' that asks, "if you had only day left on earth, how would you want to spend it? Perhaps, it's a silly question, but its worth spending some time thinking about it.

How I die is so very important. Here's Why?

How I die is so very important because it will be my last thought and my last feeling in this life.

How I handle the turmoil of my existence is going to determine my placement in the realms of Spirit when I leave here. So they become very, very important.

The life I have been living up to this point on the planet has been a rehearsal for death. So, I have to know how to get away from the body cleanly. I have to know where I am going to place my consciousness.

That is why the fifteen day journal is very, very important to my spirituality. The more I dwell upon Allah and Allah's love and the extension of that consciousness to me. When it comes to those last moments before I leave, my thoughts will be on that.

And to that is where I will go. Most of us are afraid of dying. But when I can contact the Spirit inside of me, I find peace, and death seems as natural as breathing. I look death in the face, and this frees me to focus on life.

While death is stalking me, I am stalking Spirit. Seeking God in every moment of life is called stalking the Spirit. I constantly show love for God, who loves me always. I also stalk death by rehearsing my last words:

"I did the best I could, YA Allah!"

I do only what will bring me closer to Allah regardless of an distractions.

I've now reduced my own life to just one thing. Seeking Allah 24/7. I do this through a process repeating YA Allah, YA BUB—I've done the best I Could.

Repeating this *affirmation* (**Mantra**) has revealed to me the 'secret'—of *the importance of coming into alignment.* I let the Right Side of Spirit move me with its knowledge and wisdom.

Sometimes, it warns me ahead of time, and other times it just walks me into a situation and see how I handle it! I've no separation between my mind, body and emotions.

In closing, let me say this that over the past few years, my own work and personality have come under heavy criticism by some people who do not agree with what I was doing.

Some people in my monthly group meetings and seminars seemed to be anti-experiment and I have always been pro-experiment, trying new ideas and approaches to any spiritual concepts.

For me the best response to all these people has been to live happily and successfully regarding of what has been said or done. I have endeavored to live my life internally, without attachment to the world or to what other people say, do or even think.

We are each an extension of Allah and, as such, we have certain attributes in common with Allah. One is the power of creation. Part of our experience on the physical plane is to become a consciously aware and responsible creator, and to create those things that are positive.

The Soul, in Itself, is both positive and negative. It is complete in its energy pattern. Seeing Myself as Soul, in the way I use the term here simply means bridging the Left and Right Sides of Spirit.

If I take the Left Sided Spirit in my one hand, and the Right Sided Spirit in the other, and brought the Spirit together so that they touch, I will still have the Left Side and the Right Side Spirit.

But I began to merge them I will have the new Spirit—called –Soul in the middle. This new blend in the middle is the point of convergence.

This point of convergence is, for lack of proper words: **Seeing Myself as Soul.**

The key to remember is that both sides of Spirit are necessary to maintain balance and seeing myself as Soul. When I am moving in the same direction as Spirit, I am aligned, my convergence point shifts and I am able to hold it by observing it.

*****

SELECTIONS FROM THE SAYINGS AND PREACHINGS OF IMAM ALI IBN ABU TALIB, INCLUDING HIS REPLIES TO QUESTIONS AND MAXIMS MADE FOR VARIOUS PURPOSES.

Excerpt from the book: NAHJUL BAKAGA by Imam Ali ibn Abu Talib

16. Amir al-mu'minin, peace be upon him, said: "All matters are subject to destiny, so much so that sometimes death results from effort

*****

My Favorite Sayings of Imam ibn Abu Talib.

Excerpt from the : NAHJUL BALAGHA by Imam Ali ibn Abu Talib

17. Amir al-mu'minin, peace be upon him, was asked to explain the saying of the Messanger of Allah (God) **that:** Banish your old age (by hair-dye) and do not acquire resemblance to the Jews. **Amir al-mu'mninin replied:**

"The Prophet (p.b.u.h.a.h.p.) said at the time when religion was confined to a few, but now that its expanse has widened and it is firmly settled everyone id free in his action."

The intention is that since in the beginning of Islam the number of Muslims was limited it was necessary to keep them distinct from the Jews in order to maintain their collective entity, so Prophet ordered the use of hait-dye which was not in use among the Jews. Besides, it was also the aim that when facing the enemy the people should not look old in age and weak.

19. Amir al-mu'minin, peace be upon him, said: "He who gallops with loose rein collides with death."

20. Amir al-mu'minin, peace be upon him, said: "Forgive the shortcomings of considerate people because when they fall into error Allah (God) raises them up."

24. Amir al-mu'minin, peace be upon him, said: "To render relief to the grief-stricken and to provide comfort in hardship means the atonement of great sin."

28. Amir al-mu'minin, peace be upon him, said: "The best abstemiousness is to conceal it.

29. Amir al-mu'minin, peace be upon him, said: "When you are running away from the world and death is approaching, there is no question of delay in the encounter."

30. Amir al-mu'minin, peace be upon him, said: "fear! Fear! By Allah (God), He has hidden your sins so much so as though He has forgiven."

31. Amir al-mu'minin, peace be upon him, said: "The doer of good is better than the good itself, and the doer of evil is worse than the evil itself."

33. Amir al-mu'minin, peace be upon him, said: "Be generous but not extravagant; be thrifty but not miserly."

34. Amir al-mu'minin, peace be upon him, said: "The best of riches is the abandonment of desires."

35. Amir al-mu'minin, peace be upon him, said: "If someone is quick in saying about people what they dislike, they speak about him that about which they have no knowledge."

36. Amir al-mu'minin, peace be upon him, said: "Whoever prolongs his desires ruins his actions."

40. Amir al-mu'minin, peace be upon him, said: "The tongue of a wise man is behind his heart, and the heart of the fool is behind his tongue."

s-Sayyid ar-Radi says: "This sentence has a strange and beautiful meaning. It means that the wise man does not speak with his tongue except after consulting his mind and exercising his imagination, but the fool quickly utters whatever comes to his tongue without thinking. In this way, the tongue of a wise man follows his heart while the heart of the fool follows his tongue."

41. This very sense has been related from Amir al-mu'mnin, peace be upon him, in a different version as follows:

"The heart of a fool is in his mouth while the tongue of a wise man is in his heart.

44. Amir al-mu'minin, peace be upon him, said: "Blessed is the person who kept in mind the next life, acted so as to be able to render account, remained content with what sufficed him and remained pleased with Allah (God)."

45. Amir al-mu'minin, peace be upon him, said: "Even if I strike the noise of a believer with this, my sword, for hating me he will not hate me, and even if I pile all the wealth of the world before a hypocrite (Muslim) for loving me he will not love me. This is because it is verdict pronounced by the tongue of the revered Prophet, may Allah bless him and his descendants -, as he said: *O' Ali", a believer will never hate you and a hypocrite* (Muslim) *will never love you."*

46. Amir al-mu'minin, peace be upon him, said: "The *sin* that displeases you is better in the view of Allah than the *virtue* which makes you **proud.**"

47. Amir al-mu'minin, peace be upon him, said: "The worth of a man is according to his courage, his truthfulness is according to his balance of temper, his valor is according to his self-respect and his chasteness is according to his shame."

48. Amir al-mu'minin, peace be upon him, said: "Victory is by determination; determination is by turning over of *thoughts*, and thoughts are *formed* by guarding secrets."

49. Amir al-mu'minin, peace be upon him, said: "Fear the attack of a noble person when he is hungry, and that of an ignoble person when he is satiated.

50. Amir al-mu'minin, peace be upon him, said: "The hearts of the people are like wild beasts. Whoever takes them, they would pounce upon them."

51. Amir al-mu'minin, peace be upon him, said: "So long as your position is good, your defects will remain covered."

52. Amir al-mu'minin, peace be upon him, said: "The most capable of pardoning is he who is the *most* powerful to punish."

53. Amir al-mu'minin, peace be upon him, said: "Generosity is that which is by one's initiative, because giving on being asked is either out of self-respect or to avoid rebuke."

54. Amir al-mu'minin, peace be upon him, said: "There is no wealth like wisdom, no destitution like ignorance, no inheritance like refinement and no support like consultation."

55. Amir al-mu'minin, peace be upon him, said: "Patience is of two kinds, patience over what pains you, and patience against what you covet."

56. Amir al-mu'minin, peace be upon him, said:" Contentment is wealth that does not diminish."

as-Sayyid al-ar-Radi says: "*This saying has also been related from the* Prophet*, may Allah (God) bless him and his descendants.*

Contentment means that a man should remain satisfied with what he gets and should not complain if he gets less. If he is not so contented he will try to satisfy his greed by committing social crimes like cheating and misappropriation and deceiving others, because greed compels one to satisfy one's wants by any mean whatever. Then the satisfaction of one's want opens the way for another want and as a man's wants get satisfied his craving increases and he can never get rid of his needs or of dissatisfaction. Contentment makes a man carefree from all wants except the most essentials ones. This is that everlasting wealth that gives satisfaction for good.

SERMON 49

Excerpt from the: NAHJUL BALAGHA
by Imam Ali ibn Abu Talib

SERMON – 49 About Allah's (God) greatness and Sublimity:

"Praise be to Allah (God) who lies inside all hidden things, and towards Whom all open things guide.

He cannot be seen by the eyes of an onlooker, but the eye which does not see Him cannot deny Him while the mind that proves His existence cannot perceive Him.

He is so high in sublimity that nothing can be more sublime than He, while in nearness, He is so near that no one can be nearer than He.

But his sublimity does not put Him at a distance from any of His creation, nor does His nearness bring them on equal level to Him.

"He has not informed (human) wit about the limits of his qualities. Nevertheless, He has not prevented it from securing essential knowledge of Him."

So He is such that all signs of existence stand witness for Him till the denying mind also believes in Him."

Speaking for myself, there are two things that stood boldly before me in this Sermon of Imam Ali ibn Abu Talib.

First, God cannot be seen by the eye of an onlooker, but the 'eye' which does not see Him cannot deny him.

I believe that what Imam Ali is saying here is that our physical senses reflect our physical awareness, and our spiritual senses reflect our spiritual awareness.

We cannot have the spiritual awareness with our physical senses and vice versa. Just as we need the physical eyes to see the physical things, we also need the spiritual eye (called the third-eye).

People who have spent a life-time in spiritual pursuits instead of reacting to the material world say that the spiritual eye is located in the center of the forehead. It is referred to as the pineal gland of the brain by anatomists.

Perhaps, that is what Imam Ali ibn Abu Talib is referring to the 'third-eye within us which sees God and cannot deny. It is not my intent to elaborate on the 'third eye' because most modern libraries are full on this subject. My only intent here is that Imam Ali ibn Abu Talib had this spiritual knowledge and shared it with us.

The second thing that stood boldly before me in this Imam Ali's Sermon was: **"He has not informed** (human) **wit about the limits of his qualities.**

Nevertheless; He has not prevented it from securing essential knowledge of Him."

I believe that no-one on the surface of the earth knows more about the limits of God's qualities than Imam Ali ibn Abu Talib. I say this because the **NAHJUL BALAGHA** is a living proof of the validity of God's limit of His qualities, it contains 236 SERMONs, 79 LETTERS, Selections from 489 sayings and preaching of Imam al-mu'mnin 'Ali ibn Abu Talib (p.b. u.h.) including his replies to questions and maxims made for various purposes.

So—what are the limit of his qualities of God that He has not prevented it from securing essential knowledge of Him? You may ask: "I found my answer NAHJUL BALAGA, in the description of the Creation of Adam.

Here is what Imam Ali says: *Allah* (God), *collected from hard, soft, sweet and sour earth, clay which He dripped in water till it got pure, and kneaded it with moisture till it became gluey.*

"From it He carved an image with curves. Joints, limbs and segments. He solidified it till it dried up for a fix time and a known duration.

Then He blew into it out of His Spirit whereupon it took the pattern of a human being with mind and governs him, intelligence which makes use of, limbs that serve him, organs that change his position, sagacity, that differentiates between truth and untruth, taste and smells, colors and species. He is a mixer of clays of different colors, cohesive materials, divergent contradictories and differing properties like heat, cold, softness and hardness."

What all that means in plain language is that Allah collected from hard, soft, sweet and sour earth, clay which He (Allah), mixed with some key or main Spirituals elements that would enable each and every human being capable of securing *essential knowledge* of God. Just think of it!

That key element, that main element is called (for lack of proper word) SOUL! The thing to remember is that: Soul, is to human being is what Spirit is to God. Soul is essentially synonymous to Spirit (Allah).

For example, if you have a large glass of water and you pour Some in a small cup, what will you have in the cup? You'll still have the same water but, in a small container. The same way, as Imam Ali says: *"Allah blew into it out of his Spirit whereupon it took the pattern of a human being."* Very simply stated, *We as human being are a part of the Spirit* (Allah), *but in a small container* (the physical body). So—you might say that I'm a Spiritual being having a physical experience here on earth. I am, in reality a Soul.

*****

AFTERWORD

In the Parable of Ali, Prophet Mohammed (p.b.u.h.) **Says:**

> *"I am the city of knowledge, and Ali*
> (p.b.u.h. *is the door, of that city."*

Knowing Myself as Soul

The word *Soul*, in the way I use here throughout in this book refers to my ***becoming consciously aware of my-self as a Soul and as a one with Allah not in theory but a living a reality in my own life.*** My spiritual teacher called it ***Soul Transcendence.***

For me, this glimpse of my own *awareness* of my-self as Soul came as an act of 'grace'. I really experienced this 'awareness' as the separation of the thinking of my mind, and becoming aware of my own mind's thinking. I was totally awake, totally alert, not thinking of anything or asking for anything. My own mind was quiet as if the mind is dead (so to speak) and without any thoughts. In the East it's called the 'no-mind'.

All those who have intuitively experienced this 'state-of-mind' do agree with me that this experience of the *awareness* of

145

something in the mind without any thoughts, is a divine part of who I am—I call this *awareness* within my-self, for lack of proper words—my Soul.

This was indeed an awakening process for me that took thirty-five years to manifest through me.

I suddenly, realized that Soul is one of the divine part of Spirit. The division between the two sides of Sprit is so delicate, it can take years of experience to learn to recognize the subtle energies emanating from the two sides.

And, many people deafen themselves to Spirit for lack not awareness and lock themselves into the left side of consciousness, and cutting off the possibility of the movement of Spirit. These energies emanating from the two sides of Spirit do not obey any rules.

It's up to me to use them to advance my spiritual intention. It is important to see where the alignment energies are coming in. Alignment with Spirit is ongoing challenge. My own intention sets my direction, and as long as I am moving in the direction of my intention, I am doing all I need to—just do what I can.

One thing I've learned is that when I become *aware* of my-self as a Soul and as a one with God—not in theory but a reality in my daily life then, I become aware of my permanent relationship with God, and how God's love is always in favor of life rather than death. It is said that the greatest quality or attribute of God is *love*.

His divine love for us cures all physical ailments often without knowledge. ***Knowing my-self as Soul has cured the pain in my back spine and enabled me to avoid major back surgery and loss of left foot.*** A few years ago, through my own stupidity and mistake I hurt my back by lifting a very heavy book shelf by myself. (We forget that we are not as young as we were used to be 20 years ago).

An MRI scan showed a herniated disc in my lower back spine. My neurosurgeon I visited for the treatment of my back pain suggested that the back surgery was urgently needed to cure my severe lower back spine pain.

The surgeon further wrote in his evaluation report that if I did not consider immediate surgery on my left foot at once, and if I waited too long for the operation, I might not regain the use and strength of my left foot. In other words, without the operation I might lose my left foot for good. The thought of losing my left foot for ever surely scared me, to say the least.

The neurosurgeon has certainly did a good job of instigating fear of losing my left foot in my mind if I did not act on his diagnoses of operation. He had caused anxiety, depression, and mostly the emotions of guilt and doubts for not considering the only option for surgery to save my left foot. I'm a border-line diabetic and take my sugar pills twice a day.

Everything is under control but, now with this neurosurgeon's report, I was somewhat confused and I will tell you why?

My spiritual teacher has taught me that during my meditation I should withdraw my Intention within and put it on the 'third-eye' to open it and connect it with the Pineal gland of brain to activate it.

Then, visualize that there is a door at the center of your chest and concentrate on it and imagine this door wide opens and the heart opens and suddenly bright, beautiful, divine LIGHT enters the heart through the back SPINE and 'connects' with 'third-eye' in the head and direct it to the forehead (behind the eyebrows) out into the universe and the internal becomes the external.

My spiritual teacher emphasized the fact that the 'third-eye' is truly responsible for many healing processes in my body and the heart actually heals your body.

To make the long story short, I began to keep the 'third-eye' open as much as possible 24/7 and I engaged my own 'heart-chakra' and imagined **Connecting heart with body and** see my body through the heart-energy, I saw the body as a perfectly healed body.

I visualized by body as already healed and without any pain. Sure enough, lo and behold, my body began to heal as if there no pain. The swelling on my left foot began to recede and I was able to want normally again without the fear of losing my left foot.

On my next visit to the neurosurgeon, I confidently told him that I believe that there was a Higher-power within me that can and did heal my ailment, and at this time I do not want to consider surgery.

The following story shows that God's love for each human being, actually heal the body and it reveals, to my own satisfaction at least, the *love* of life drives each soul. As you read this story, I believe that you'll observe that while you are reading it, you were somehow lifted to a higher sense of mental and spiritual elevation.

In all honesty, within this story, I did find the 'secret', knowing myself as a soul and as a one with God not, just in theory but a living reality in my own life. It is called ***Soul Transcendence.*** This story is about a talk Dr. Richard Cabot, the dean of Harvard Medical School had given to the Massachusetts Society (MMS). It seemed that Dr. Cabot had been involved in an autopsy of a man who had been killed instantly in a fatal auto accident.

The man whom Dr. Richard Cabot did the autopsy was a man who, as they often, say, was never sick for a day in his entire life. In fact, he never ever took a day off from his work for any illness or sickness.

Dr. Cabot ad the his team of medical experts while doing the autopsy on that man discovered, that this man had massive scar tissues within his body. The scar tissues showed that his body had experienced ***and did heal itself*** from all sorts of health problems, including cancer, and various other illnesses. ***The*** *doctor said that at the very moment of his autopsy, this man had four other fatal and other unusual diseases in his body.*

And, the man had never been aware of it. Dr. Cabot, in his autopsy report to the MMS, said that; *somehow, something in this man's body system had set-up a sort of a 'defense' against these four fatal and unusual diseases in his body.* As a direct result of this autopsy, Dr. Cabot went on to consider the possibility, every human being has this 'healing' power within.

Dr. Cabot decided ultimately to report his conviction to the Massachusetts Medical Society that this inner-wisdom, this Higher-power within all of us is always biased in favor of life over death.

He then, went on to admit most of our health problems, difficulties, diseases or ailments that we have throughout our lives, we never know about or even experience in our outer life.

This is, Dr. Cabot said, because of the tremendous, 'healing-power' of this energy which is actively working on our behalf within all of us. (this invisible, inner 'higher-energy' within us the doctor is referring to the Spirit—God).

Dr. Cabot had been shocked, and had undergone a certain amount research as a direct result of this autopsy, and discovered some insights into this invisible, 'higher-energy' within us, and his finding had certainly shocked his colleagues and confidants. Dr. Cabot went on to say that this power-full 'healing-energy' (referring to the Spirit), is ten times as powerful as any medicine available to mankind on Earth.

When ask, *"What is this powerful invisible 'higher-energy' with the human body?"* Somewhat hesitant but blushing, Dr. Cabot said: *"It was God's love."*

I acknowledge God's presence by allowing it into my life without restriction or conditions.

I believe that God does not care how, where, or what It touches me, because it is not a respecter of persons and It does not care what I think about it. Whether I want the 'healing' now, last week, or in a month—It and Its own time. And, my job is to be ready to receive of God's love at any time and at all times.

For me, one easy way to be ready to receive of God's love is that I put my Intention on to the 'third-eye' (Pineal gland). I imagine it as a really small dot, a red dot, a black dot, or a purple dot or a blue.

I imagine this 'dot' inside my head as a full size eye (just the size of my eye) just inside my head. (we call it the Pineal gland) so that it's easier to kind of let my body know where I am addressing my intention.

So, finally, my 'third-eye' area is just behind the eyebrows. I sit-up straight have my feet on the ground and have my spine straightened (its important)for my visualization exercise.

I keep my feet on the ground, take a few deep breaths, and just relax. I imagine that there is door that can center over my chest and opens up and bright, beautiful, divine LIGHT enters through the 'heart-center' and travels, up to spine where it meets tat Pineal gland, where that inner-eye directs that LIGHT through my browser (behind the eyes area) and out into the universe.

So—the internal becomes the external. I do this spiritual exercise a couple of times and it take me just two minutes to do it. I do it as often as I can.

To repeat it, *My chest is open, my heart is open and the light enters through my heart up through my heart up through my spine, meets the inner-eye and travel through the browse on my forehead behind the eyebrows and out into the universe.*

I feel the sensation of the divine LIGHT traveling through my own body. With my eyes closed tight, I look up inside my forehead and see the dot (for me the dot comes in blue color), I suddenly imagine it opens up.

When it closes again, I try to open again and again. I feel a little pressure in my head and I know it is beginning to open up for me. I know it is safe and natural to open the 'third-eye' God intends for me to open my 'third-eye". When I do this process through the 'heart-energy' the heart actually heal my body I see the world through my inner-vision. *I engage my heart-chakra to connect heart with head.*

*****

Distinct Sayings of Amir al-mu'mnin,

Excerpt from the book: NAHJUL BAKAGA by Imam Ali ibn Abu Talib

58. Amir al-mu'minin, peace be upon him said: "Wealth is the fountain head of passions."

59. Amir al-mu'minin, peace be upon him said: Whoever warns you is like one who gives you tidings."

60. Amir al-mu'minin, peace be upon him said: "The tongue is like a beast; if it is let loose it devours."

61. Amir al-mu'minin, peace be upon him said: "Woman is like a scorpion whose grip is sweet."

62. Amir al-mu'minin, peace be upon him said: "If you are met with a greeting, give better greetings in return. If a hand of help is extended to you, do a better favor in return, although the credit would remain would remain who was first."

63. Amir al-mu'minin, peace be upon him said: "The interceder is the wing of the seeker."

64. Amir al-mu'minin, peace be upon him said: "The people of the world are like travelers who are being carried while they are asleep."

65. Amir al-mu'minin, peace be upon him said: "A lack of friends means strangeness."

66. Amir al-mu'minin, peace be upon him said: "To miss what one needs is easier than to beg from inappropriate person."

67. Amir al-mu'minin, peace be upon him said: "Do not feel ashamed for giving little, because refusal is smaller than that."

68. Amir al-mu'minin, peace be upon him said: "Charity is the adornment of destitution, while gratefulness (to Allah) is the adornment of riches."

69. Amir al-mu'minin, peace be upon him said:: "If what you aim at does not come about then do not worry as to what you were."

70. Amir al-mu'minin, peace be upon him said: "You will not find an ignorant person but at one extreme or other."

71. Amir al-mu'minin, peace be upon him said: "As intelligence increases, speech decreases."

72. Amir al-mu'minin, peace be upon him said: "Time wears our bodies, renews desires, bring death nearer and takes away aspirations. Whatever is successful with it encounters grief and whoever misses its favors also undergoes hardships."

73. Amir al-mu'minin, peace be upon him said: "Whoever places himself as a teacher of the people should commence with educating his own self before educating others: **and his teachings should be by his own conduct before teaching by the tongue.** The person who teaches and instructs his own self

154

is more entitled to esteem than he who teaches and instructs others."

74. Amir al-mu'minin, peace be upon him said: "The breath of a man is a step toward his death."

75. Amir al-mu'minin, peace be upon him said: "Every countable thing is to pass way and every expected thing must come about."

76. Amir al-mu'minin, peace be upon him said: "If matters get mixed up then the last ones should be appreciated according to the previous ones."

79. Amir al-mu'minin, peace be upon him said: "Take wise points from wherever they maybe, because **if a wise saying is in the bosom of a hypocrite** it flutters in his bosom till it comes out and settles with others of its own category in the bosom of the believer."

80. Amir al-mu'minin, peace be upon him said: "A wise saying is a lost article of the believer. Therefore, get wise sayings even though from people of hypocrisy."

81. Amir al-mu'minin, peace be upon him said: "The worth of every man is in his attainment."

*****

SERMON 1

Excerpt from the: NAHJUL BALAGHA
by Imam Ali ibn Abu Talib

SERMON – 1 - The Creation of the Universe.

"He initiated creation most initially and commenced it originally, without undergoing reflection, without making use if any experiment, without innovating any movement, and without experiencing any aspiration of mind. He allotted all things their times, put together their variations, gave them their properties, and determined their features knowing them before creating them, realizing fully their limits and confines and appreciated their propensities and intricacies."

"When Almighty created the openings of atmosphere, expanse of the firmament and stara of winds He flowed into it water whose waves were stormy and whose surges leapt one over the other."

"He loaded it on dashing wind and breaking typhoons, ordered them to shed it back (as rain), gave the wind control over the vigor of the rain, and acquainted it with its limitations. The wind blew under it while water flowed furiously over it."

"Then Almighty created forth wind and made its movement sterile, perpetuated its position, intensified its motion and spread it far and wide."

"Then, He ordered the wind to raise up deep water and to intensify the waves of the oceans. So the wind churned it like the churning of curd and pushed it fiercely into the firmament throwing its front position on the rear and the stationary on the flowing till its level was raised and the surface was full of foam."

"Then Almighty raised the foam on to the open wind and was vast firmament and made therefrom the seven skies and made the lower one as stationary surge and the upper one as protective ceiling and the high edifice without any pole to support it or nail to hold it together."

"Then He decorated them with stars and the light of meteors and hung in it shinning sun and effulgent moon under the revolving sky, moving ceiling and rotating firmament."

*****

The information that follows may seem rather abstract. It's okay if you don't fully understand it. Just allow your inner wisdom to absorb it. Keep reflecting on these issues suggested here. You will find your understanding of them deepening more and more as you progress the path toward God.

*****

Knowledge of the Creation by Allah.

When I was born in this world, I must have sacrificed a Spiritual World. In the Spiritual World in which I lived as Spirit, as Pure love and as a divine part of Allah.

I must have looked down into this physical world, and looking from that high pure love, I imagined doing everything with perfect love, because from the place I was looking from, everything looked perfect.

The funny thing is that everything here on earth is still perfect just the way I saw it from the high pure love on **the spiritual world above.**

Everything here on earth, indeed is still perfect just the way I saw it from the Spiritual world, the problem is that I just don't like it the way it is. So, the problem is not that the physical world is not perfect. The problem is that I need to **see it through the eyes of the Spirit**. We see the physical world through the two physical eyes and not through the spiritual-eyes (the third-eye) which is often closed due to the lack of not knowing how to open it and activate the pineal gland. Let me tell you my story of how I might have decided to be born here on earth in this physical body. I believe I must have decided t leave the **realm of Spirit in**

heaven in order to gain the experience of the rich living in this physical world and become a Co-creator with God in heaven.

I wanted to experience all levels and conditions of God. Thus, the earth experience is a part of my evolution into the consciousness of God. So,

I agreed to be born in the physical realm, but the problem was that to be born in the physical world, I was to be born in the physical body in the Physical realm in order to move down from the positive Spirit realm into the negative five realms namely: *etheric, mental, causal, astral, and of course the physical.*

The point I am trying to convey here is that The Soul, as rule is both male and female, but when I decided to be born into this physical world, I choose to come into this world this time as a male.

Also, soul, in itself is both positive and negative, not in the sense it is 'good' or 'bad' but, in the sense of the positive and negative polarity of the battery. It is complete in its energy pattern, like the Creator is complete.

To make the long story of my birth short, as Soul, I first picked up an *'etheric'* body in the human consciousness below the soul ream in the realms of Spirit. (This was the very first stage of my human consciousness).

I'm still a divine part of Spirit but not as a physical body as yet. Next I descended and picked up a mental body which covered my soul but still not in the physical form.

I then picked up the *Causal* and the *Astral* bodies in the same manner and then after up to nine months of stay as a Spirit in the body of my mother,

I ultimately picked up my own unique *Physical body* all wrapped-up in my own Soul ready to experience the rich living on earth as a human being.

The sad thing is that you and I forget that we as human beings, don't really belong here spiritually. You and I were implanted (so to speak) here in this physical body and on this physical world attempting to fulfill certain God-like qualities within ourselves, and we forget that you and I do have a prime directive;

You and I are here to find out who we are, and to find out where our home in Spirit from where we came and to where we return is, and to go there in consciousness, and to have a co-creative consciousness with our Creator Allah!

Connecting heart with head in the way I use here is simply means that as Soul, in my own human physical body, not only I as a Soul, through the human form can experience all the negative realms (etheric, mental, casual, astral and the physical), but I also can directly experience the positive (Soul and Spirit) that exist beyond the negative. The first of the positive realm is the Soul realm.

The point is that this is the very first level where I am consciously **aware of my own true nature.**, my true 'beingness' and my **oneness with Allah**.

There are many ascending realms of pure Spirit above the Soul realm.

*I pretend that **Connecting Heart with Head** is symbolic way of my own relationship with the Creator Allah, where heart represent the Spirit and the head represents the Soul.*

I sometimes indulge in my own imagination to see what kind of a place this world would be in which to live if everyone on earth could learn to open the third-eye and activate the pineal gland.

As Allah is my witness, when I do my daily meditations, I imagine connecting my heart in my physical body with the pineal gland in my brain in my head, and it connects me to the Higher Mind or the Higher Source (or whatever you want to call it).

I imagine that there is a door at the center of my chest that opens-up and suddenly the bright, beautiful, divine LIGHT enters through my heart center and travels up through my spine where the LIGHT meets with the pineal gland—the inner-eye and, the inner-eye directs that LIGHT through the area of the third-eye in my forehead and travels out into the whole universe.

So, the internal becomes the external and it makes my everyday life magical in the truest spiritual sense. I really feel the sensation, the tingle of 'heart energy' traveling though my beings.

The most amazing part of this connection is that the heart actually helps me heal myself of all the physical ailments and I begin to see the world as a happy place. I see others as divine beings, and see everything inner connected. Just think of it!

I acknowledge my own Spirit's presence by allowing *It* into my own life without restriction or conditions. I sense as if Spirit touches my heart and wants to heal me now. I am always ever ready to receive of the Spirit at any time and at all times.

I believe from the bottom of my heart that a great deal of stress, struggles, sorrows, fear and doubts is a result of not **knowing how to connect our heart with head**. We let the mind keeps us totally occupied with the past or the future. I believe that it is the cause of so many of our troubles.

You and I can't see the Soul's presence because Soul is 'wrapped-up' in the **five negative** realms of Spirit inside of us. I always tell myself that *Soul is who I am*. Soul is a divine part of *who Allah Is*. Soul keeps me alive, not the mind. Mind cannot be trusted because mind is the devil's advocate. I am an extension of the Spirit and, as such, I've certain attributes in common with the Spirit—and not with the mind. *Mind is my enemy* because it will go against me in my Spirit. But, let me be perfectly honest with you and tell you that **connecting heart with dead** is a twenty-four-hours-a-day, seven-days a-week job.

There are no vacations either, but the rewards are certainly worth it. For thirty-five long years I've been totally committed to *honesty, truth, duty and love*, and a continual demonstration of those efforts.

It wasn't easy, at least at first. But, after a while the rewards started coming in and I found **I wouldn't have any other way**. I created love, harmony, happiness, peace, these qualities began to be returned to me.

Wise Sayings of Amir al-mu'mnin.

Excerpt from the: NAHJUL BALAGHA by Imam Ali ibn Abu Talib.

83. Amir al-mu'minin, peace be upon him said about a man who praised him much, although he did not admire him: "I am below what you express and above what you feel in your heart."

87. Amir al-mu'minin, peace be upon him said: "I wonder about the man who loses hope despite the possibility of seeking forgiveness."

91. Amir al-mu'minin, peace be upon him said: "The hearts get disgusted as bodies get disgusted; so look for beautiful **wise** saying for them."

92. Amir al-mu'minin, peace be upon him said: "The most humble knowledge is that which remains on the tongue and most honorable one is the that which manifests itself through (the action of) the limbs and the organs of the body."

106. Amir al-mu'minin, peace be upon him said: "Often the ignorance of a learned man ruins him while the knowledge he has does not avail him."

107. Amir al-mu'minin, peace be upon him said: "To miss an opportunity brings about grief."

133. Amir al-mu'minin, peace be upon him said: "This world is a place for transit, not a place for stay. The people herein are of two categories. One is the man who sold away his self (to his passions) and thus ruined it, and other is the man who purchased his self (by control against his passions) and freed it."

134. Amir al-mu'minin, peace be upon him said: "A friend is not a friend unless he affords protection to his comrade on three occasions: **in his adversity, in his absence and at his death.**"

137. Amir al-mu'minin, peace be upon him said: "Seek livelihood by giving alms."

138. Amir al-mu'minin, peace be upon him said: "He who is sure of a good return is generous in giving."

142. Amir al-mu'minin, peace be upon him said: "Loving one another is half of wisdom."

151. Amir al-mu'minin, peace be upon him said: "Every human being has to meet the **end, sweat ot sour.**"

153. Amir al-mu'minin, peace be upon him said: "The endure does not miss success although it may take a long time."

154. Amir al-mu'minin, peace be upon him said: "He who agrees with the actions of a group of persons is as he joins them in that action.And everyone who joins in wrong commits two sins; **one sin for commiting te wrong and the other for agreeing with it**."

167. Amir al-mu'minin, peace be upon him said: "**Vanity prevents progress.**"

179. Amir al-mu'minin, peace be upon him said: "**Stubbornness destroys** (good) **advice.**"

180. Amir al-mu'minin, peace be upon him said. "**Greed is a lasting savery.**"

187. Amir al-mu'minin, peace be upon him said: "**The departure** (from this world) **is imminent.**"

188. Amir al-mu'minin, peace be upon him said: "Whoever away from right was ruined."

189. Amir al-mu'minin, peace be upon him said: If patience does not give relief to a man impatience kills him."

197. Amir al-mu'minin, peace be upon him said: The hearts become tired as the bodies become tired. **You should therefore search for beautiful sayings for them.** (to enjoy by way of refreshment).

217. Amir al-mu'minin, peace be upon him said: "Through change of circumstances the mettle of men is known."

217. Amir al-mu'minin, peace be upon him said: "Jealousy by a friend means defect in his love."

246. Amir al-mu'minin, peace be upon him said: "When capability increases, desire decreases."

248. Amir al-mu'minin, peace be upon him said; "Generosity is more prompting ro good than regard for kinship."

249. Amir al-mu'minin, peace be upon him said: "If a person has a good idea about you make his idea be true."

250. Amir al-mu'minin, peace be upon him said: "The best act is that which you have to force yourself to do."

252. Amir al-mu'minin, peace be upon him said: "The sourness of this world is the sweetness of the next world."

288. Amir al-mu'minin, peace be upon him said: A small action which is continued with regularity is mre beneficial than a long one performed with disgust."

290. Amir al-mu'minin, peace be upon him said: Whoever keeps in view the distance of the journey remains prepared."

291. Amir al-mu'minin, peace be upon him said: "Perception by the eyes is not real observation because the eyes sometimes deceives people; but wisdom does not deceive whomsoever it counsels."

292. Amir al-mu'minin, peace be upon him said: "Between you and the preaching there is a curtain of deception."

293. Amir al-mu'minin, peace be upon him said: "The ignorant among you get too much while the learned are just put off."

294. Amir al-mu'minin, peace be upon him said: "knowledge dispels the exchuse of those who advance excuses."

304. Amir al-mu'minin, peace be upon him, was asked about the distance between East and West when he replied: "One day's traveling for the sun."

305. Amir al-mu'minin, peace be upon him said: "Your friends are three and your enemies are (also) three. **Your friends are :** your friends, your friends's friend and your enemy's enemy. **And your enemies are:** your enemy, your friend's enemy and your enemy's friend,"

306. Amir al-mu'minin, peace be upon him, saw a man busy against his enemy with what was harmful to himself too, so he said: "You are like one who pierces spear through himself in order to kill the person sitting behind him."

315. Amir al-mu'minin, peace be upon him said: "A self-respecting man **never** commits adultery."

323. Amir al-mu'minin, peace be upon him said: "Qur'an contains news about the past, foretelling about the future and communications for the present.

324. Amir al-mu'minin, peace be upon him said: "Throw a stone in return from where one comes to you because evil can be met only with evil."

336. Amir al-mu'minin, peace be upon him said: "The age up to which Allah accepts any excuse for human being is sixty years."

345. Amir al-mu'minin, peace be upon him said: "There are two shares in the property of every person—success and accidents."

346. Amir al-mu'minin, peace be upon him said: "The person who is approached with a request is free until he promises."

352. Amir al-mu'minin, peace be upon him said: "The biggest wealth is that one should not have an eye on what other possess.

372. Amir al-mu'minin, peace be upon him said: "He who is jealous of his esteem should keep from quarrelling."

374. Amir al-mu'minin, peace be upon him said: "Do not ask about things which may not happen because you have enough to worry about with what happens."

375. Amir al-mu'minin, peace be upon him said: "Imagination is a clear mirror, and the taking of lessons (from things around provides warning and counsel. **It is enough for improving yourself that you should avoid what you consider bad in others."**

376. Amir al-mu'minin, peace be upon him said: "Knowledge is associated with action. Therefore, he who knows should act, because knowledge calls for action; if there is a response well and good, otherwise it (i.e. knowledge) depart from him."

396. Amir al-mu'minin, peace be upon him said: "One who is in search of something will obtain it, at least a part of it."

402. Amir al-mu'minin, peace be upon him said: "Speak so that you may be known, since man is hidden under his tongue.:

404. Amir al-mu'minin, peace be upon him said: "Many an expression is more effective than an attack."

407. Amir al-mu'minin, peace be upon him said: "The best scent is muck; its weight is light while its smell is scentful."

408. Amir al-mu'minin, peace be upon him said: "Put off boasting, give up self-conceit, and remember your grave."

409. Amir al-mu'minin, peace be upon him said: "The child has a right on the father while the father too has a right on the child. The right on the father on the child is that latter should obey the former in every matter save in committing sins of Allah, the Glorified, while the right of the child on the father is that he should give him a beautiful name, give him good training and teach him the Qur'an."

411. Amir al-mu'minin, peace be upon him said: "Nearness with people in their manners brings safety from their evil."

413. Amir al-mu'minin, peace be upon him said: "whoever hankers after contraries gets no means of success."

418. Amir al-mu'minin, peace be upon him said: "Whoever clashes with Truth would be knocked down by it."

419. Amir al-mu'minin, peace be upon him said: "the heart is the book of the eye."

422. Amir al-mu'minin, peace be upon him said: "It is enough for your own discipline that you abstain from what dislike from others."

423. Amir al-mu'minin, peace be upon him said: "One should endure like free people, otherwise one should keep quite like ignorant."

442. Amir al-mu'minin, peace be upon him said: "Remember that pleasures will pass awa while the consequences wit stay."

456. Amir al-mu'minin, peace be upon him said: "Whoever trades without knowing the rules of religious law will be involved in usury."

458. Amir al-mu'minin, peace be upon him said: "Whoever maintains his own respect in view, his desires appear light to him."

459. Amir al-mu'minin, peace be upon him said: "Whenever a man cuts a joke he separates away a bit from hit wit."

460. Amir al-mu'minin, peace be upon him said: "Your turning away from him who inclines toward you is a loss of your share of advantage while your incline toward him who turns away from you in humiliation for you."

466. Amir al-mu'minin, peace be upon him said: "Two greedy persons never get satisfied, **the seeker of knowledge and seeker of this world.**"

467. Amir al-mu'minin, peace be upon him said: "Belief means that you should prefer truth (even) when it haems you rather than falsehood (even) when it benefits you; that your words should be more than your action and that you should fear Allah when speaking about others."

469. Amir al-mu'minin, peace be upon him said: Forbearance and endurance are two twins and they are the product of high courage.

470. Amir al-mu'minin, peace be upon him said: "Backbitting is the tool of the helpless."

480. Amir al-mu'minin, peace be upon him said: "There is no good in silence over matters involving wisdom just as there is no good in speaking with ignorance."

486. Amir al-mu'minin, peace be upon him said: "The worse sin is that which committer takes lightly."

*****

Notes from Mushtaq Haider Jaafri:

This is the end of our selection of the few select Sayings, and the Letters and of the utterance of Imam Amir Ali al-mu'mnin, peace be upon him. I am indeed, praiseful to Allah (God) the Glorified, for having enabled me to collect and to bring together from different places of the material from the book: NAHJUL BALABA - Peak of Eloquence by Imam Ali ibn Abu Talib.

SERMON 187

Excerpt from the: NAHJUL BALAGHA
by Imam Ali ibn Abu Talib

SERMON – 187…. Allah's favors

"I advise you, O' people, to fear Allah and to praise Him profoundly for His favors to you and His rewards for you and His obligations on you."

"See how He chose you for favors and dealt with you with mercy. You sinned openly; He kept you covered. You behaved in a way to incur His punishment, But He gave you more time."

Condition of person facing death

"I also advise you to remember death and to lessen your heedlessness toward it. Why should you be heedless toward Him who is not heedless of you?"

"Why expect from Him (i.e., angel of death) who will not give you time? The dead whom you have been watching suffice as preachers.

They were carried to their graves, not riding themselves, and were placed in them but not of their own accord. It seems as if they never lived in this world and as if next world had always been their abode."

"They have made lonely the place where they were living, and are now living where they used to feel lonely. They remained busy about what they had to leave, and did not care for where they were to go."

"Now, they can not remove themselves from evil, nor add to their virtues. They were attached to the world and it deceived them. They trusted it and it overturned them."

Transience of this world

"May Allah have pity on you. You should therefore hasten towards (the preparation of) houses) which has been commanded to populate, and toward which you have been called and invited."

"Seek the completion of Allah's favors on you by exercising endurance in His obedience and abstention from His disobedience, because tomorrow is close to today."

"How fast are the hours of the day, how fast the days in a the month, how fast the months in the year and how fast the years in a life."

*****

SERMON 190

Excerpt from the : NAHJUL BALAGHA
by Imam Ali ibn Abu Talib

SERMON – 190 – Praise of Allah

"Praise be to Allah Whose praise is wide-spread, Whore army is over-powering and Whose dignity is grand.

I praise Him for His successive favors and His great gifts. His forbearance is high so that He forgives and is just in whatever He decides.

He knows what is going on and what has already passed. He crafted all creation by His knowledge and produced it by His intelligence without limitations, without learning, without following the example of any intelligent producer, without committing any mistake and without the availability of any group (for help).

*****

Sermon 197

Excerpt from the: NAHJUL BALAGHA
by Imam Ali ibn Abu Talib

SERMON – 197…. Allah's attributes of Omniscience.

"Allah knows the cries of the beasts in the forest, the sin of the people in seclusion, the movement of the fishes in the deep sea and the rising of the water by tempestuous wind."

"This Islam is the religion which Allah has chosen for Himself, developed it before His eyes, preferred it as the best among his creations, established its pillars on His love."

*****

SERMON 202

Excerpt from the : NAHJUL BALAGHA
by Imam Ali ibn Abu Talib

SERMON – 202 – Transience of this world, and importance of collecting provisions for the next world.

"O' people, certainly this world is a passage while the next world is a place of permanent abode. So, take from the passage (all that you can) from for the permanent abode."

"Do not tear away your curtain before Him Who is aware of your secrets. Take away from this world your hearts before your bodies go out of it, because herein you have been put on trial, and you have been created for the other world."

"When a man dies people ask what (property) he has left while the angels ask what (goof actions) he has sent forward. May Allah bless you; send forward something, it will be a loan for you, and do not leave everything behind, for what that would be burden on you."

SERMON 211

Excerpt from: NAHJUL BALAGHA
by Imam Ali ibn Abu Talib

SERMON – 211 – About those who gave up supporting right.

"O' my Allah! Whoever listen to our utterance which is just and which seeks the prosperity of religion and the worldly life and does not seeks mischief, but rejects it after listening, then he certainly turns away from thy support and desists from strengthening Thy religion."

"We make Thee a witness over him and thou art the greatest of all witness, and we make all those inhabit Thy earth and thy skies witness over him"

"Therefore, Thou alone can make us needless of his support and question him for his sin."

*****

SERMON 218

Excerpt from: NAHJUL BALAGHA
by Imam Ali ibn Abu Talib

SERMON – 218 – Qualities of the God-fearing and the pious.

"**He** (the believer) **kept his mind alive and killed** the desires of) **his hear till his body became thin, his bulk turned light and an effulgence of extreme brightness shone for him.**"

"**It lighted the way for him and took him on the** (right) **path.**"

"**Different doors led him to the door of safety and the place of** (his permanent) **stay. Hid feet, balancing his body, became fixed in the position of safety and comfort, because he kept his heart** in good acts) **and pleased his Allah.**"

*****

SERMON 223

Excerpt from the: NAHJUL BALAGHA
by Imam Ali ibn Abu Talib

SERMON – 223 – Supplication.

"O' my Allah! Preserve (the grace of) my face with easiness
of life and do not disgrace my countenance with destitution,
lest I may have to beg a livelihood from those who beg from
Thee, try to seek the favor of thy evil creatures, engage
myself in praising those who give to me, and be tempted in
abusing those who do not give to me, although behind all
these thou art the master of giving and denying."

"Verily Thou over all things, art the All-powering.
(Qur'an. 66.8)

*****

SERMON 225

Excerpt from the: NAHJUL BALAGHA
by Imam Ali ibn Abu Talib

SERMON – 225 – …Supplication.

"O' my Allah! Thou are the most attached to Thy Lovers and the most ready to assist those who trust in thee."

"Thou seest them in their concealment, knowest whatever is in their consciences, and art aware of the extent of their intelligence."

"Consequently, their secrets are open to Thee and their hearts are eager from Thee. If loneliness bores them,

Thy remembrance give them solace. If distress befall them, they beseech Thy Protection, because they know that the reins of affairs are in Thy hands, and that their movements depend upon Thy command."

"O' my Allah! If am unable to express my request or cannot see my needs then guide me toward my betterment, and take my betterment and take my heart toward the correct goal."

"This is not against (the mode of) **Thy guidance nor anything new against Thy ways of support.**"

"**O' my Allah!** *Deal with me through Thy forgiveness and do not deal with me according to your justice.*"

Notes from Mushtaq Haider Jaafri:

This ends of our selection of the few select Sermons, Sayings, Letters and the utterance of Imam Amir Ali al-mu'mnin, peace be upon him. I am indeed, praiseful to Allah (God) the Glorified, for having enabled me to collect and to bring together from different places of the material from the book: **NAHJUL BALABA**

Peak of Eloquence by Imam Ali ibn Abu Talib translated by Sayed Ali Raza and included introductory note by Sayed Mohamed Askafy Jafery. This original book consists of 680 pages of Sermons, Letters, and Sayings of Imam Ali ibn Abu Talib. It is recommended that all Muslims of the world read this book at least once in your life.

The information that follows may seem rather abstract. It's okay if you don't fully understand it. Just allow your inner wisdom to absorb it. Keep reflecting on the issues suggested here. You will find your understanding of them deepen more and more as you progress of the examples of chaste language.

*****

Recently, I was working with a worldwide organization called the *Movement of Spiritual Inner Awareness (MSIA)* which is based, in Los Angeles, California. This movement was begun more that fifty-five years ago by a man named **John-Roger** who held the inner-keys to the mystical traveler consciousness. John Roger once said something in his seminars that truly caught my attention and I would like to share with you because it talks accepting mind as an enemy. *John-Roger use to say:* "Your thoughts and feelings will shake you harder than anyone else can shake you. That is why your mind is your enemy because it will go against you in your Spirit.

Accepting Mind as an Enemy

A spiritual master I was working with once asked me: Can you accept an enemy and say: "I love you?" I often heard him say to others that: "I love you if you love me. And, I love you if you kill me." These are very powerful statements. I really didn't understand the true meaning of what the master was say.

Then, suddenly, it dawned on me that once I truly embrace the enemy, it turns to help me. Then I don't have stubbornness, I have determination. This transformed the moment I accepted it, and all the power that was blocking me before now becomes of ascension, of uplifting.

The master taught me that once I accept the enemy and once I embrace it, that enemy will transform and yield its power to me.

Then, the master said: "I'm referring to accepting the enemy within—which is your own mind."

He said; your own thoughts, your emotions, and your feelings will shake you harder than anyone else can shake you. That is why your own mind is your enemy because it will go against you in your Spirit.

And, it seems to win because although your Spirit, the Soul is the Spiritual warrior, the mind is the physical armored warrior who will attempt to destroy any chance of ever spending more time in your spiritual pursuits and make you re-act to material world. You will find dealing with all 'petty-tyrants" in your daily life, bugging you with impurity.

So be sure to identify the petty-tyrants in your own life, past or present. Some of our spouses and kids seemed to be expert in this field. They will hit your hot buttons. The key to all this is observing your own thoughts instead of reacting, or fighting them during your meditation.

I observe the thoughts that come into my mind. I notice that the more I observe my own thought in my mind, the more they begin to subside and eventually leave the mind. For me one easy way to open that pineal gland of my brain and activate it for connecting the heart with head is to sit in an easy chair.

I take a few deep breaths, and focus on my own breathing and as I begin to do that I begin to put the awareness more within—as an observer mode rather than an reactive mode. When I am in that meditation, I just observe the thoughts that come in. I don't judge them as good or bad, happy or unhappy, or resist them.

I just continue to observe them.

The funny thing is that the more I observe them they begin to go away from the mind naturally almost as I am not fighting them. The reason all thoughts begin to go away is because I am not giving them energy. And, as those thoughts begin to go away and then I focus on relaxing my eyes, my face.

Then, I close my eyes and when I close my eyes I begin to raise my brain waves from the beta level to the alpha level where my own mind start to generate mostly more *alpha* waves, more relaxing waves in the pineal gland of my brain and I am shutting-off (so to speak) my two physical eyes, and opening my spiritual-eye (third-eye).

Then, with my own two eyes closed, I begin to focus moving my eyes almost *up look at my forehead* behind the eyebrows. I am looking at the imaginary third-eye in the size of my full eye, on my forehead.

I see totally darkness there and lo and behold, a tiny purple dot appears and I know that my: third-eye is in the process of opening and activating the pineal gland in the brain.

The point I am trying to convey here is that as I close my physical eyes, and look upward into the dark area of my forehead behind the eye brows, what I am symbolically doing is doing is that I am literally putting my focus on the third-eye which is closed at the moment and then I decide that as I am putting the intention on the closed third-eye—it suddenly opens-up and I do this over and over again until someday, it does open up for me.

Most people claim that with persistence and patience and practice it does open-up The only question is that how much you want it to open-up and how much practice with persistence you are willing to do it.

And, as I do that I begin to put the awareness within and begin to experience the connection with the higher source to which I am connected already. For me, this experience, this awareness, this connecting heart with head comes as a sensation, as a tingle or some kind of pressure in my head.

It is something visual, or feeling inside my head and as I begin to do that I begin to tap-in to more of that energy, more of that connection that already exists now but cluttered up by the reactive mind. How long, then, it takes to learn to open the third-eye and activate the pineal gland in the brain? It depends upon you.

If you love and trust in God, then you'll find the process to be an easy skill to master. All it takes is to observe the mind-activity without being involved in it. Spiritual masters of all ages call observation the key to letting go.

When something unpleasant, something disturbing shows up, and you just begin to observe it without reacting emotionally to it, you will notice with profound interest that you don't ever get thrown off balance.

Only human beings are capable of observing the presence of Alah in all things including us.

Recently, I did a Google-search for How to Open the Third-eye and Activate the Pineal Gland. To my surprise and amazement, more than 415,000 hits showed up on this particular Google-search. I even found the internet loaded with spiritual people offering techniques how to open the third-eye and activate the Pineal gland of the brain.

Apparently; this is exact the kind of information people who are spiritual and not necessarily religious were looking for. You see, religious is traditions and rituals *we do.* Spiritual is something *we are.*

There is a difference because you can be a very religious person, and not be spiritual—and vice Versa.Spiritual Masters of all ages who have spent a life-time in spiritual pursuits instead of reacting to the material world affirm that we as human beings are a spiritual beings having a physical experience here on earth.

We are SPIRIT—a divine part of God. We are the essence of who God Is. Just think of it! The funny thing is that many spiritual people are offering various techniques how to quickly and safely open the third-eye and activate the Pineal gland of the mind.

Some of these Google-searches have several millions hits on the Google-search. It does prove to me, at least to my own satisfaction anyway, that we as a human race are ready and willing to accept that we are not here to do what we know how to do. We are not here just to learn what we already know.

We are here to learn what we do not know and what we do not know how to do which is I believe, learning to open the third-eye and activate the Pineal gland of the brain to find out who we are and to find out where the Soul realm is and to go there to have a co-creative consciousness with God in heaven.

This is the way how I see our existence here.

What I mean is that we don't belong here—spiritually! Perhaps, that is why we have such a hard time fulfilling our spiritual promise here on earth and making ourselves do what we want to do according to our intention, because our intention only works best in the Spirit.

I earnestly believe from the bottom of my own heart, that our creator has given each human being three special and unique gifts that no other creation by God has been given. I call these three gifts from God the *awareness of inner spiritual movement* because they allow me to observe the presence of God in all things, including myself. Human beings are sacred because of the three gifts from our creator.

If only we could understand that simple fact, we would never need to read another self-help book! How can we observe God when we are observing outside where it can never be found.

All spiritual teachings say: The kingdom of heaven is within. The Bible it says: "Seek first the kingdom of Heaven:

So—what are those three special and unique gifts that every human have? You may ask: My answer.

The first gift is the *intention*. I mean, we as human beings have the God-given power and the privilege to put our intention wherever we want to.

The second gift is *concentration*. We can put our concentration on anything or anyone or anywhere we want to. *Please remember that I don't mean focus, but concentration because there is a difference. Focus is just to see or look.* Concentration is going beyond focus.

It the separation of thinking of the mind and your awareness of the mind's thinking without being any part of the mind's thinking.

In the East, it is called the *awakening process*, or a mind without any thoughts or a no-mind. It proves that we are *not* the mind. We are Spirit—a Soul. The third gift is the *imagination*. None of the creation by God has been given this special and unique gift of imagination. The power of imagination is awesome and is responsible for the comforts and making everyday life magical, to say the least.

The sad thing is that we, as a human race, have advanced enormously technologically, but as a race we are still doing the same destructive things that were reported in the biblical days thousands of years ago.

I believe that although, we have advanced tremendously in the material world, we are still in the 'stone-age' spiritually.

I believe human race is shifting in consciousness now where we are ready and willing to open the third-eye and activate the Pineal gland in the brain to make a connection with the higher Mind, or Higher Source (or whatever you want to call it). My Google-search proved this fact, at least to my own satisfaction.

As I go about my daily business, I try to put my own *intention* inside my head on the Pineal gland in my brain (third-eye). I concentrate on the third-eye-area on my forehead behind the eyebrows.

Using the power of *imagination* I then, imagine that there is a 'door' on the center on my chest that opens-up, and I visualize, or imagine or just pretend that the bright, beautiful, divine LIGHT, enter my heart—and travel through my back spine upward in my head and meets the 'third-eye' which direct the heart-energy through the third-eye-area of the forehead and browse outside the whole universe and the internal becomes the external and I sense as if I've become aware of myself as a Soul and as a one with God not just in theory but a living reality in my daily life. *It takes me just two minutes to do it.*

I do this meditation as often as I can and anywhere and anytime I can. Just think of it. Anytime, I am stuck on the freeway traffic waiting for it move forward, guess, what I do. Yeah—I take a few deep breaths.

I put my intention on the 'third-eye' I concentrate and the bright, beautiful, divine Light entering through my spine and meeting the third-eye which directs the heart energy through third-eye are behind the eyebrows outside the universe and connects with the universal mind or the source for experiencing myself as a Soul and as a one with God as a living, breathing reality in the world.

I do the same meditation if I am sitting alone in my car for a long time wait my family to do shopping or whatever. I do this meditation 24/7 day in and day out. I've now reduced my own life to just one thing: Seeking God 24/7.

I do this through a process I learned from my spiritual teacher who revealed to me the three gifts of Allah.

The most amazing thing about this quick meditation is that it helps me align myself with God. This short meditation has revealed to me the secret that inside of me who I am as a Spirit meets the Soul who is there temporarily. Here the Spirit, the divine part of who I am meets me.

The spiritual masters of all ages calls it 'the point of convergence'. This short meditation has assisted me in converging my spirit back into alignment.

My Soul is what keeps me alive, not my mind. Mind as strong as it may sometimes seem to be, is just vehicle for connecting heart with head. Mind can be constructive if used rightly but it can be very destructive if used wrongly. Mind is the enemy within and I accept it as such.

Accepting the enemy within in the way I use here refers to the two aspects of the left and the right sides of the spirit. Our mind plays a devil's advocate in the left side of the spirit.

Finally, let me say this that one of the Pineal gland of the brain is to look more deeply at *who I am* and *what I am about.* I take some time to look within myself and see *who is there*—and I've truly found the true me, and I am truly living that life. What's more I really don't care whether I live or die because that part of me will never die and always exists. You might say that I live from the outside in. Doing my daily meditations,

I've been able to open up sort of a passageway between my Soul and the Spirit by opening the third-eye and activating the Pineal gland of my brain. I always try to catch myself thinking. You might say I've become a 'mind-watcher'.

I have spent more than thirty-five long years reading every book that I could lay my hands on, hoping to come to a deeper awareness of God. Like most of the people I know, I too had my own preconceived ideas of what the Spirit, or the Divine, or God look like.

Unfortunately, to my dismay, after spending all these long years in the spiritual pursuits, I discovered that the reality of God cannot be learned through study. I discovered that the only way I can discovered God is through direct experience inside of me.

Spiritual masters of all ages confirm that the Spirit does not care whether you want to align with it now, last week, or in a month—it moves on Its own way and Its own time.

And, my job is be ready to receive the Spirit. Perhaps, that is why the Spirit is ruthless—in a nice way. Spirit does not care where, or when, or how it touches me. But, I can tell you one thing. It is all well worth the wait once the Spirit did touch me.

For me, one thing is for sure, *Allah is unknowable—but, I know Allah!*

Just think of it!

*****

Afterword

An Excerpt from the talk:
Who are the Shia Muslims
By Mustafa Al-Qazamini

In the Parable of Ali, Prophet Mohammed (p.b.u.h) **Says:**

"I am the root, Ali is the branch, Hasan and Husain are the fruit and Shias are the leaves."

> "Allah has not informed
> (human) wit about the limits
> of his qualities. Nevertheless,
> He has not prevented it from
> securing essential knowledge
> about him."

Coming into Alignment

"Inside us, who we are as an eternal being meets the person who is there temporarily here. Here the Spirit, the emanation from God meets us, the selves we know. This is our point of convergence.

A pint of concentration or intention. The Spirit can be converge inside is in many ways. Someone yelling at us can change our convergence. When Spirit and mind move to the right, we can be very irritated and yell back.

But when they move to the right, we say "Aha!" We see events of the moment more clearly, and new ideas come forward, often quite rapidly. An essential part of our training—*spiritually—is recognizing when this takes place.*

If we can change our spiritual consciousness, we can move toward the convergence point. We can spend more time in spiritual pursuit instead of just reacting to the material word.

We can remain at peace. We can never control God, but we can— *align* an flow with His will."

"It is a tremendous thing to have no separation between your Spirit and your mind, emotions, and body. Then there will

be just one Spirit coming into convergence and alignment with the unknowable energy we call Allah."

"Once you decide to keep moving forward, you will devise a method to chart your progress. And gradually you will begin to move from the left to the right sides of Spirit, and when you come to the middle, everything starts to come closer to you.

It comes towards you as you go toward it, ultimately, to convergence and Alignment We can view it as predestined, and in a sense it is. Remember that both sides are necessary to maintain the balance of Spirit. .

The division between the two sides of the Spirit is so delicate, it can take years of experience to learn to recognize the subtle energies emanating from the two sides.

When convergence point shifts and you are able to hold it, you open up new Perspective, awareness, and insights. Spirit is ruthless, not out of malice, but out of purposefulness. Spirit does not stop to accommodate us. We follow Spirit.

How do we know if we are aligned with Spirit?

"We can learn to recognize when we are aligned and when we are not: Physically, not being aligned will feel and look like tension; being grumpy, emotionally, like upset; being very reactive and impetuous, speaking without thinking, mentally, like resistance,. words and actions are not in line.

Start to change the neurological and physiological patterns. See where the alignment energies are coming in. These energies don't obey any rules; it's up to you to use them to advance your spiritual intention.

Alignment with Spirit involves detachment from the world; but ir does not mean hatred of the world. *The joy of alignment flows over everything you do, including the most mundane aspect of your day-to-day life.*

How few people realize that it is actually easier to live in alignment through the right side, by loving, caring, and sharing. *You automatically touch others. You don't have to search them out or puzzle over how to help them. It just takes place.*

This is not to say that alignment with Spirit is not an ongoing challenge. But remember, your intention sets your direction, and as long as you are moving in the direction of your intention, you are doing all you need to."

"The only this that you can take with you—the only thing that is going to live, and never die—is the Soul. *You must get this one intention very clear, :I'm keeping my eyes on you, Lord, only you."*

That means I am only doing the things that bring me closer to the Lord regardless of any distractions that may present themselves. Are you starting to see how precious is the time you've already had? And, how much more precious is the time that remains to you? Keeping death in mind is not being morbid. It's being aware that you do not have time to waste.

In the world of Spirit there is no time. But you are still here and you are living. Time is precious. This physical world can act as springboard for you into the higher consciousness. Our bodies, minds, emotions, unconscious and Soul come together in one place giving us the best opportunity in the universe for growth and upliftment. So in these last few days of living, use your time for your advancement. Practice dying every day and experience rebirth at every minute, This is not physical death, but willingness to see everything anew in each moment.

*****

To Sum up!

Finally, please allow me to close this book by saying that I've learned what it takes to become *aware* of myself as a Soul and as a one with God not in theory but a living reality in my daily life.

Over the past few years, my own work and personality have come under heavy criticism by some people who didn't agree with what I was doing.

Many people have asked me, "By what authority do I speak?' After all, I am not Scholar, or a Moulana, or Reverend or anyone "official." Yet, I could ask, "By what authority do you question."

The "authority" to question and to speak out is both inherent within each one of us. I say what I say because I can. Many people never do speak out because they don't trust themselves or are afraid of the reaction of others.

When we are not aligned with our Soul, we need the outside world to validate our religious or spiritual positions. We want something "official: to tell us we are on the right track.

This is a form of spiritual immaturity, and hold us back from our best selves.

As we become spiritually immature, we attune to our Soul nature. We participate. We see that the world is the screen upon which we project ourselves, so we see flaws out there, we are the ones who need to change. And this change can only come by discovering our true nature, the Divine within us.

Interestingly enough, in my own life's journey, unconsciously, I've regularly gone back to this book **NAHJUL BALAGHA** by Imam Ali ibn Abu Talib to be reminded of *Allah has not informed* (Human) *wit about His qualities. Nevertheless, He has not prevented it from securing essential knowledge of Him.'*

I believe this Allah's promise took me to many other spiritual paths beyond my own religion of Islam as a Shia Muslim, to get check them out and secure the essential knowledge first hand.

This book attempts to share with you that essential knowledge I have learned. I know they work, because I have tried and tested all these principles time and time again in my own life.

Since I am a practical man, this is a practical book. I have endeavored to live my life internally, without attachment to the world. "How do you securing essential knowledge of the qualities of Allah? My answer: Read the NAHJUL BALAGA!

ABOUT – MUSHTAQ HAIDER JAAFRI

He came to the United States of America as a foreign student in order to acquire a higher education. It was his father Mr. Nazir Ahmad Jaafri who sent him to California for his higher studies.

It was his father's vision for knowledge, which gave him the opportunity to find the only fortune worth finding, a 'seed' of greatness which God plants in every one of us. His father's vision gave Jaafri a direct path to God and that touch of Greatness that God plants inside every one of us.

"You are the architect and builder of your own life", his father often said. He holds advanced degrees in communication and in the field of metaphysics. He is the published author of seven books in the field of 'mind-conditioning' techniques using a unique system of thought control. **(available at www. amazon.com).**

He was mentioned in Who's Who in Metaphysics. His latest book, was written after 30+ rears of deliberate monitoring of his own thoughts on a daily basis. He was willing to sacrifice anything and everything but, not his God-given right and the privilege of controlling his own thoughts at all costs.

Based on his own personal experiences in trying to quiet the conscious thinking mind, he discovered and pioneered the 'mind theory' of five features of the mind and the function they serve for Soul to use them as 'vehicle' to communicated with other minds. By utilizing the Soul Travel techniques he was able to go beyond the ego's incessant compulsive thinking at will whenever he wanted.

This deliberate monitoring of his own thoughts on a 24/7 basis, he was able to open up sort of a 'passage way' between Soul and his True-Self or God-Self, thus blending of Human and Divine personalities within.

His high goal of experience himself as Soul, not in theory but as a reality in life is what this new book is all about He has truly caught of the essence of the amazing MIND BYPASS techniques, so his very fitting writing in this new book NAHJUL BALAGA is a reminder of this journey toward spiritual freedom.

Contact the Author

MUSHTAQ HAIDER JAAFRI
919 Sonora Ct,
San Dimas, CA 91773
mushtaqjaafri@gmail.com

Go with the Flow! A Way to Blissful Living

By: Rev. Dr. Mushtaq H. Jaafri
Publisher: AuthorHouse
Publication Date: February 2017
ISBN: 978-1-5246-7064-1
Reviewed by: Amy Lignor
Review Date: March 13, 2017

When it comes to the arena of self-help/inspirational books, there are far more than 84 of them. However, this actually helps you understand the "wheel of 84," among other practices, and how to achieve a spiritual mindset.

What does this mean, exactly? It is a fact that in Hindi, Urdu and Punjabi there is an object called a "lakh" that represents one hundred thousand units – this represents (or keeps track of) the 84 hundred thousand rounds of birth and death that a soul passes through.

However, this particular book offers 'inside information' on how to best attain a life that allows you to bypass this constant wheel.

In this highly informative book, Rev. Dr. Jaafri begins with an introduction to what the soul really is and why we should acknowledge and understand the fact that a human being is not just a physical being or physical body. We are actually all souls or spirits that are not just a theory that is written about in religious texts: our souls are a reality.

It was this informed man who felt as if his own spirit was trying to communicate with him for quite some time during his life. He went through stages of feeling "odd," perhaps even a little crazy – as we all do when we suggest to others a reality that they may not believe in or see a need for. Joining various spiritual organizations on his quest for the inner soul, Rev. Dr. Jaafri went on to learn more, communicate and actually "see" that inner spirit that made up a substantial part of him.

This book speaks about what a soul really is and how to identify with it. How we can attain a "quiet mind" that allows us to accept our souls which then allow us to "go with the flow" and accept who we are in reality.

Readers learn about this man's first look at America and how he went on to walk his own spiritual path – not with blind faith, mind you, but a path that an individual can test and "try on for size." He speaks about having faith in daily experiences and how to know that you are on the right spiritual path.

Educationally, he goes step-by-step through the mental exercises that can be done to monitor your thoughts, as well as offering answers to questions regarding the five parts of the human mind outlined in his book. He also delves into the human being's three personalities: ego self, personal self and spiritual self.

In summary, this author offers up an easy-to-understand, and even easier way to practice and accept, how to allow your spirit to be a large part of your daily life and your daily adventures.

Quill says: Among the many titles on the market in this genre, this is one that is extremely deserving of a place on your bookshelf. (Available: www.amazon.com.)

FQ: This country has hit a turbulent time in the world of politics. Do you have an opinion on how, perhaps, people could be helped and calmed by spiritual teachings?

JAAFRI: As I read this question, suddenly, a famous quote by a world's famous poet by the name RUMI, flashed into my mind. He said: "This too shall pass.

"In the Bible we read "Let God make perfect in you." It's very true, this country has hit a turbulent time in the world.

The worse I've seen during the pass half a century I've been here. The whole world used to look up to this country. In my humble opinion, the only way it could be helped and clamed is the way we learn to stop the wheel of 84.

Here is a direct quote from the MSIA founder John-Roger, DDS that could help in this country's turbulent time and help calm by keeping in mind these three things as we go through life, and they are our guidelines:

THREE GUIDELINES TO FOLLOW!

Excerpt from John-Roger—Founder MSIA.

1. Don't hurt yourself and don't hurt others.

2. Take care of yourself so you can take care of others.

3. Use everything for your uplifting, growth, and learning. (Fulfilling Your Spiritual Promise by MSIA founder John-Roger).

FQ: You mentioned Emerson in your dedication. One of the questions readers like to have answered by an author is:

"If there was one person (historical or president-day) you could sit and have lunch with and discuss everything from writing to the spiritual, who would it be and why?"

Is there one specific question you would like to ask them?

JAAFRI: The name that comes to my mind right now is Dr. Paul Kaye, DSS, the President of MSIA who encouraged me to train for becoming the MSIA Seminars Leader hosting the Soul

Awareness Seminar in my local community to teach people in regard to Soul transcendence.

Dr. Kaye took John-Roger's lecture and skillfully recognized the book: Spiritual Warrior— The Art of Spiritual Living. The funny thing is that for thirty-nine plus years, I've been living the Spiritual Warrior life-style and wrote my.

A Point of Focus:

Imam Ali ibn Abu Talib says in his book

NAHJUL BALAGHA:

"Although, Allah (God) has not informed (human) wit about the limits of His qualities; nevertheless He has not *prevented* (human) from securing essential knowledge of Him (God)." Sometimes, we may need to think outside of the box (so to speak) to secure essential knowledge of God.

What I mean is that securing essential knowledge of *Allah* (God), no matter how beautiful or poetic, is just information, *until you experience it.* When you experience it, *you know,* and no one can take it away that knowledge from you.

So—how do you go about experiencing the existence of *Allah* (God)? Well, I can only suggest what has worked for me for thirty-five years.

So-here are the five key elements that helped me experience the reality of Allah from just information and knowledge of *Allah* to a living reality in my own l daily life.

1. As a human beings I am not merely a physical body but I'm in essence a Soul or a Pure Spirit., a Divine part of God.

2. I am aware of myself as a Soul and as a one with God not in theory but a living reality in my daily life.

3. I am an awareness behind the thinking of my own mind and my own awareness of the mind's thinking.

4. I control my own mind just by "observing" my mind-activity 24/7 using Positive affirmations until there is no-mind or mind without thoughts.

5. Practice converging my Spirit back into alignment. The joy of alignment flows over into everything I do—including the most mundane aspect of my day-to-day life.

One sure way for me to know I'm experiencing the reality of *Allah* (God) within me is that suddenly I sense or feel as if I'm lifted to higher level of mental and spiritual elevation,

I sense the presence of God within me, it is just a kind of 'knowing' my own 'oneness' with a higher power of God-force with me. *It is an awareness of my spirituality through my physical individuality.*

As I go about my daily business, I suddenly become aware of myself as a part of an 'energy' or force or Spirit within me. it is as if I'm one with all things and all things are one with me.

All those who have intuitively experienced this 'oneness' with God do agree with me that it is as if you are one with nature, all things living and whole universe. You see the world through an awareness of the Spirit.

Imam Ali ibn Abu Talib says: "Allah (God) **has not informed** (human) **wit about the limits of His qualities. Nevertheless' He has not prevented it from securing essential knowledge of Him."**

I literally spent thirty-five years in securing essential knowledge of Allah. All I can say is that: *Allahis unknowable—but, I know Allah.* What I've found is the out of the unknowable comes *spiritual alignment for all of us on this planet.*

Our *intention*, **as a seeker of the knowledge of Allah, is to** *get into alignment*. **And how does it come about? Not in knowing but in** *awareness*. **We come into awareness of the unknowable. But, how can we become aware of it? By coming into alignment with it.**

The Left and Right Sides of Spirit

The sad thing is that it took me more than thirty-five years to know that Spirit is two-headed coin (so to speak). In the left and the right sides of Spirit, we find the dark (Satan) and the light (Noor) and both sides are necessary to maintain balance.

The division between the two sides of Spirit is so delicate, it can take years of experience to learn to recognize the subtle energies emanation from the two sides. And so many people deafen themselves to Spirit and lock oneself into the left side of consciousness. (I should know, I deafen myself for thirty-five years).

The funny thing is that *alignment with Spirit* involves detachment from the world; but it does not mean hatred of the world. *The joy of alignment flows over into everything you do, including the lost mundane aspects of your day-to-day life.*

"How few people realize that it is easier to live in alignment through the right side, by loving, caring, and sharing."

You automatically touch others. You don't have to search them out or puzzle over how to help them. It just takes place.

This is not to say that alignment with Spirit is not an outgoing challenge. But remember, your intention sets your direction and as long as you are moving in the direction of your intention, you are doing all you need to do.

**Everything is
information
Until you experience it.
When you experience it**

you know it
And no one can
take that
Knowledge
from you!

I've talked a lot about securing essential knowledge of Allah and experiencing it. When we are experiencing it, we are in that place that I call purity—purity of thought, of emotion, of content.

In that moment of feeling good, that moment of experiencing, the power of Allah will move inside you. You're asking, *is this some kind of phenomenon?* Absolutely!

And once you get a taste, you will be hooked: Hooked not only on your high, but also on your low, because that, too, is part of this energy of Allah. Experiencing Allah is the process that releases us and opens us and expands us to let the Spirit flow through us.

As Allah is my witness, for thirty-five plus years, I've experienced the awareness of God within me 24/7, and I can tell you firsthand that it is as part of me as my breathing.

The Joy of Alignment

The joy of my alignment through the right side of Spirit flows over into EVERYTHING I do—including the most mundane aspect of my day-to-day life.

How few people realize that it is actually easier to live in alignment through the right side, by loving, caring, and sharing. You automatically touch others. You don't have to search them out or puzzle over how to help them, it just takes place.

Your intention sets your direction, and as long as you are moving in the direction of your intention, you are doing all you need to.

There is no need to make excuses, no need for apologies, just do what you can do. It's amazing how one man's experience can touch us all.

*****

On page 213 – 216 is an excerpt from the **Feathered Quill** Book Review of **Go With the Flow! And an on-line interview of the author Mushtaq Jaafri.**

DISCLAIMER

In writing about spiritual concepts, I have inevitably used words than mean different things to different people, depending upon either the personal spiritual path they have taken or their spiritual or religious upbringing. In the pages that follow, I've words like "Soul," "soul," "Spirit," "spirit," "Self," "self," "God," Allah," and others in specific ways. To get the most out of this book, may I suggest readers (both Muslims and non-Muslims) suspend, as much as possible, their personal interpretations of these words and concepts and stay open to how I define them in context, by my explanations, by their own intuitive sense. This book is a reflection of my own spiritual understanding of the subject under discussion. It isn't intended to speak for any other modern-day religion or spiritual paths. For thirty five years I've been on my own personal spiritual path and have worked under several (non-Muslims) spiritual Masters, to get the teachings first hand. I believe that all religions ultimately lead to one Creator (God). I also believe that you can be a very religious person and *not* necessarily a *spiritual* person and vice versa. A spiritual master I was working with said: ***Religion is traditions and rituals—we do!*** But, ***spiritual is who we are.*** I've experienced myself as a Soul and as a one with God ***not*** just in theory but, a living reality in my daily life. For me, the *awareness* of God came to me as a *'sense –of- knowing'* or an 'inner-feelings' that came to me as an *'awareness'* of the **un-knowable.** I come into *awareness* of God by coming into *alignment* with it. (the left and the right sides of Spirit).

A TRUE CONFESSION!

I've talked a lot about how to have *experience with Allah* in ways that has absolutely nothing to do with the religion of Islam, and you might be inclined to believe that perhaps, I am no longer the Shia Muslim of Imam Ali ibne Abu Talib. (p.b.u.h) or his teachings and that isn't true.

Please rest assured that I am still a Shia Muslim, the follower of Imam Ali ibn Abu Talib teaching. In fact, I am an active, senior member of the Zainbia Islamic Society in Pomona, California.

For me, **NAHJUL BALAGHA** is a manual of practical spirituality about how to bring about peace and centeredness to my life no matter what challenges I am presented with.

Each Sermon, Letter and saying of Imam Ali ibn Abu Talib reinforces my habits of empathy and enthusiasm in my life and affirms and strengthen what is best in me.

I have experience with Allah, I realize that Allah is existence, and in reality I don't live Allah, as much Allah lives me. I've regularly gone back to this book to be reminded of what is so easy to forget.

LET
HUMAN
CONSCIOUSNESS
AWAKEN
EVERY SOUL
WILL utter
HUSAIN
IS mine!

Printed in the United States
By Bookmasters